In Ephraim's Footsteps

In Ephraim's Footsteps

The Story of the Three Houses of Israel

By
Clay McConkie, Ph.D.

BONNEVILLE BOOKS ™
Springville, Utah

ISBN: 1-55517-733-6
e.1

Published by Bonneville Books
Imprint of Cedar Fort Inc.
www.cedarfort.com

Distributed by:

Cover design by Nicole Cunningham
Cover design © 2004 by Lyle Mortimer

Printed in the United States of America
10 9 8 7 6 5 4 3 2 1

Printed on acid-free paper

Library of Congress Control Number: 2003114912

Note

Although much has been said about the House of Israel, there has been relatively nothing about the existence of three separate Houses by the same name, each with its own set of characteristics and circumstances. Yet in regard to this illustrious family and organization, it definitely is one which has a past, present, and future, including not just several thousand years of world history, but a much larger span comprising *premortal life, earth life,* and the *hereafter.*

Table of Contents

Part Three
A Latter-day Interlude

Part Four
The Third House of Israel

Introduction

The Three Houses of Israel

With the commencement of the resurrection three days after the death of Jesus, the three Houses of Israel came into existence. For the first time in the long span of history covering pre-earth, earth, and post-earth life, three separate and distinct organizations were in full operation, all functioning independently and at the same time.

Of course, it might be stated that there was still just one house by the same name, operating in three different stages or time periods. Yet in a very real sense, there are now nevertheless three, each one with its individual set of conditions and circumstances, and each very different from the others.

In the first place, many Israelite people in the premortal life are still waiting for a transfer to earth, some scheduled to come before the Millennium and some after. Second, an assembling of people of the same lineage is taking place in world society today, consisting of those who accept certain rules and commandments and are willing to be gathered. And finally, there are those who have already met the necessary qualifications for celestial living and eternal life and following death have been resurrected and admitted into the Celestial Kingdom.

Three Houses of Israel, therefore, exist simultaneously, but at separate levels or spheres and according to different time reckonings. All of them at one time or another have exhibited high levels of spirituality. And yet the first two still remain very tentative, their members not having been completely tried and tested. The third House only, as far as a long-range program is concerned, is the only group that might be regarded as a permanent House of Israel. Only in this last organization, which has residence in the Celestial Kingdom, is there a guarantee of Israelite citizenship that will continue forever.

This last group, being the third station in mankind's progress and development, is both the time and place where eternal life begins, the final destination for those who regain the presence of the Father and the Son. Here in the very center of the universe, at a distant location near the planet Kolob, faithful men and women reach a rendezvous point where they realize a long-awaited goal and destiny. In this place, until a celestialized earth later becomes their permanent heaven, the long journey of a covenant people finally comes to an end.

And so it is that the story of the three Houses of Israel is also brought to a close. From premortal life to earth life to resurrection in the Celestial Kingdom, the account of Israelite people moving across a vast territory of time and space finally reaches a conclusion. Those sent forth on a mission to earth return home again with honor. Certainly in no other phase of human history is there a more important and meaningful story.

All who have been in these famous Houses, carrying out heaven's plan, constitute a very unusual society, being of the same lineage or background and sharing a common goal and purpose. Each person possesses a royal heritage. Whether descended from one of Jacob's twelve sons or any of their righteous progenitors, it is always the same as far as the name of Israel is concerned. Everyone is potentially a king or a queen, a priest or a priestess, in a kingdom. All are chosen subjects of the Most High.

And yet among all of these, there is still one particular name which has a unique and special meaning, in many ways standing out above the rest. In a very significant way it is representative of all Israelite history and of the House of Israel itself.

It is the name of the man who was born in Egypt many centuries ago, far from his father's homeland in Palestine, and who, despite his Israelite ancestry, was as much Egyptian as he was Hebrew. His life, in fact, was oriented more toward the standing of a prince than a shepherd or herdsman, and one also that was very close to the throne of Pharaoh himself. Yet at the same time, and for some unknown reason, he was chosen to be the elite person among all of his Israelite brethren, the one who was given the family birthright and who inherited the prestigious title of firstborn.

Surely this was Ephraim, son of Joseph and Aseneth and a descendant of the patriarch Abraham. This was the man who was placed ahead of his older brother Manasseh and declared to be the preferred son. He also was the one whose numerous posterity became a great people and a multitude of nations, passing through many generations and eventually producing a society in the last days that initiated the vast movement of gathering. Again this was Ephraim, who symbolically has been at the head of the Israelite people from the beginning, even back to the time of premortal life, and in whose custody today is the operation and general management of the entire House of Israel!

Part One

The House of Israel in Premortal Life

Formation of a Kingdom

In the beginning, even before the creation of the earth, there was the House of Israel. Long before the time of Abraham, Isaac, and Jacob, when the famous house supposedly began, there was an earlier people who bore Israel's name.

They might not have been called such in the place where they used to be. But in a premortal existence, the lifetime before this earth, they apparently were regarded as a separate and distinct group that later was to be known as the children of Israel.

During that early time period, earth's inhabitants lived as spirit children of God. It was there that each person had the opportunity to grow and develop, to fashion for himself or herself an individual character and personality, and to prepare for an earth life that lay ahead.

It was also a time when there was war in heaven. Michael and his angels, who represented the views of deity, fought against Satan and his angels. Billions of people took sides in a dispute, and as a result Satan and a third part of the people in heaven were cast out.

Down through the ages of premortal life, men and women had progressed to a point where they were ready to go through the experience of earth life and mortality. But because of a difference of opinion as to how things should be done, a conflict arose, and all who supported Satan were banished from heaven forever.

Among those who remained, which was the huge majority of the people, there was general agreement, but also a wide range of intellect and ability. All agreed with the plan for beginning earth life, and yet because of the many different levels of human development, everyone would not be starting out under the same conditions. Especially in regard to spirituality, one part of heaven stood out noticeably above the rest and would be given extra preference. This was the House of Israel!

As a just reward for achievement and obedience, these people were to receive and be placed in personal circumstances on earth that generally would be more favorable for their spiritual development. The idea was to use earthly experience not only to gain a physical body but to develop personality and intellect as well, especially as they related to religion and the degree of spirituality which would ensure an eventual return to the kingdom of heaven.

The House of Israel, therefore, was an elite group, a kingdom within a kingdom, composed of those who had been most valiant in pre-earth life. They were the ones who potentially would be foremost on earth in promoting righteousness and carrying out heaven's plan. All were in the institution in heaven that the Lord would later characterize as an unusual people as he spoke to the children of Israel when they came out of Egyptian bondage.

He told them on that occasion,

> Now therefore, if ye will obey my voice indeed, and keep my covenant, then ye shall be a peculiar treasure unto me above all people: for all the earth is mine: and ye shall be unto me a kingdom of priests, and an holy nation.[1]

Certainly this was an unusual group, and from among its most prominent members in premortal life came the ecclesiastical leadership, including the Lord Jesus Christ at the head, and others such as Adam, Enoch, and Noah, as well as Moses and Abraham. And besides these, all of whom were chosen beforehand, there were many more, such as the prophets Isaiah and Jeremiah. The latter, in fact, at the very beginning of his ministry, referred specifically to himself as having an earlier lifetime and calling.

> Then the word of the Lord came unto me, saying, Before I formed thee in the belly, I knew thee; and before thou camest forth out of the womb I sanctified thee, and I ordained thee a prophet unto the nations.[2]

Along with religious leaders, men and women in other fields were also undoubtedly chosen in advance. Based upon talent and capability, along with obedience and faithfulness, a huge structure of leadership was established in heaven long before it materialized on earth, people coming from many different segments of society, both within and outside the House of Israel. A large number of those selected, in other words, especially the ones qualified in areas such as politics, economics, and the arts and sciences, would logically come from other groups in addition to those known as Israelites.

The important thing was to prepare for the future, and also to reward those who were ready for positions of leadership. Clearly it was a matter of choosing the right individual for the right kind of mission. In regard to religion, these people were often clearly defined, one of them being the patriarch Abraham who was recognized by the Lord as being one of the noble and great ones among premortal spirits and, as in the case of Jeremiah, was chosen to be a prophet before he was born.[3] But at the same time there were many others whose circumstances were not so clearly defined.

Two of these, for example, were Jacob, also known in the Bible as Israel, and one of his many grandsons whose name was Ephraim!

Jacob and Ephraim

The usual way of describing the House of Israel's origin is to associate it with Jacob, the second son of Isaac and the grandson of Abraham. It was Jacob whose name was changed to Israel and who had twelve sons, each of whom became the head of a tribe. These sons and their descendants then became known as the twelve tribes of Israel.

Although the famous house had actually begun much earlier, far back in premortal life, it was not until the time of Jacob that it was identified by name as an earthly institution. He was the one, by way of an unusual and controversial blessing, who became its beginning patriarch and progenitor. It was also during his lifetime that the Israelites commenced a new era in their history, leaving the land of Palestine and journeying into Egypt.

In a normal situation, however, things might have turned out very differently. It could have been Esau, for example, the firstborn son of Isaac and Rebecca and Jacob's twin brother, who was the original progenitor. Because he was slightly older and traditionally entitled to the birthright and a special blessing, he was the person who logically might have originated the twelve tribes.

And yet things were never planned that way! Before Esau and Jacob were ever born, the Lord himself made it known as to which child had been chosen over the other. He told their mother,

> Two nations are in thy womb, and two manner of people shall be separated from thy bowels; and the one people shall be stronger than the other people; and the elder shall serve the younger.[4]

In very few places in the Bible is it stated more clearly that important matters on earth are first planned in heaven. Especially in the case of Jacob and Esau, the idea of foreordination and selection exists as a very important principle. It might not always be apparent at first, but it is there. Even Isaac did not know what was happening, for example, in regard to his two sons, and had it been left up to him alone, Esau would have probably received the greater blessing.

Still another example of foreordination was when Ephraim received an important calling instead of Manasseh. Both were sons of Joseph and the grandsons of Jacob, and although Manasseh was older and technically deserved the birthright, it was the younger brother once again who was given the preferential blessing.

On one occasion just before Jacob died, he blessed both of his grandsons and told them they would each develop into a great people, but that Ephraim, whose posterity was to become a *multitude of nations*, would be greater. Again it was a matter of things being decided ahead of time in heaven. Joseph did not know what was taking place, but to some degree, at least, Jacob did, and for the first time Ephraim was established as someone of great prominence on earth, one who had a unique and unusual destiny.[5]

Later this prominence was further enhanced when he ascended to the forefront of all the tribes and for an unknown reason was given the exclusive status of *firstborn* for the entire House of Israel, in addition to a share of the birthright which he already held with his brother.[6] The youngest of all the tribal leaders was designated as one whose descendants down through the centuries would be important representatives and fulfill a significant role of leadership.

Of course, it was not Ephraim himself who was so important at the time, but rather the lineage which he introduced, the long line of posterity that would come after him. It was also an instance once again which showed the extensive planning that must have occurred during what has come to be known as premortal life.

Premortal Callings

One of the ways of knowing what took place during an earlier time period in connection with the House of Israel is to look at the premortal lifetime of Jehovah, or Jesus Christ. He was the firstborn of the Father, meaning that he was the first to enter heaven as a spirit child of God. After him came billions of others, male and female, many of them possibly in order according to their obedience and intelligence.

Very little is known about the kind of existence that preceded that time, but as to the life in heaven which followed, there are certain clues and information. In the Gospel of John, for example, in the New Testament, it is stated that before Jesus was born on earth, he was with his Father and had already attained the level of Godhood. It was during that time that he was schooled and prepared for an earthly ministry.

Jesus often referred to this relationship with his father, including the glory which he had with him before the beginning of the world.[7]

> He that sent me is true and I speak to the world those things which I have heard of him."

> "I do nothing of myself; but as the Father hath taught me, I speak those things.[8]

At one time, after being criticized for healing someone on the sabbath day, Jesus made it clear that he was only doing that which his Father would have done. "The Son can do nothing of himself," he said, "but what he seeth the Father do: for what things soever he doeth, these also doeth the son likewise."

He then told them that they would yet see greater things, even people being raised from the dead, something which he also learned from his Father![9]

Others besides Jesus probably received this same kind of training and instruction, except at a different level, in preparation for their own future callings. Men such as Adam, Enoch, and Noah, along with Moses and Abraham, all were undoubtedly schooled in their various responsibilities. Their memory and recall on earth would not be as great as that of Jesus, but they would still have a special aptitude and potential for carrying out the Lord's work.

An important principle in all of this, of course, is agency and freedom of choice. Even though a person was foreordained and called to a certain position in premortal life, he or she still was free to accept that calling on earth or reject it, although the inclination would be to do one more than the other.

This apparently was true in the case of Jacob who had an advantage over his brother Esau. The latter chose to marry Caananite women against his parents' wishes, and his brother could have done the same. But Jacob had been given a blessing, which was based upon a previous foreordination, and his inclination on earth was to accept it. He then went on to marry within the chosen lineage and eventually became a great prophet and patriarch.

In regard to the two brothers, Jacob undoubtedly was the one who had been more faithful and obedient during a previous lifetime, which explains why he got the blessing. Had it been Esau who had been more faithful, things might have happened in a more usual way.

The same also must have been true with Ephraim and Manasseh. Ephraim had evidently excelled in premortal life, for example, and had gained preference over his brother. Consequently, he received a higher status during earth life and was given the coveted birthright, not only within his own family where Joseph was the father, but for the entire family and House of Israel!

Foreordination and Election

The callings of Jacob and Ephraim, like those of many others, came about as the result of two important principles: *foreordination* and *election*. Men as well as women, because of their ability, obedience, and past performance, were foreordained in heaven to be given certain duties and responsibilities and then called and elected to carry them out. Both of these principles were outlined by the Apostle Paul in the New Testament.

In his epistle to the Romans, for example, Paul referred to the concept of predestination, also interpreted as foreordination. Referring to the Father, Paul said,

> For whom he did foreknow, he also did predestinate to be conformed to the image of his Son, that he might be the first-born among many brethren. Moreover, whom he did predestinate, them he also called: and whom he called, them he also justified: and whom he justified, them he also glorified.[10]

In the same area of scripture, Paul stated that people were called according to God's personal knowledge and purpose. In other words, the Lord knew in the premortal life who it was that was capable, as well as dependable, and these were the ones he chose for future discipleship and leadership. It might be that others would come forth on their own volition, but the intent was that those called and elected would be at the forefront.

Paul illustrated this point when he talked about the birth of Jacob and Esau. "And not only this," he said, in writing to the Romans, "but when Rebecca also had conceived by one, even by our father Isaac . . . it was said unto her: the elder shall serve the younger." He clarified his statement by saying that it was the purpose of God, through the principle of election, to place Jacob ahead of Esau.[11]

Once again, it was the idea of choosing, and also rewarding, those who had excelled in premortal life, not only the noble and great ones, but all who had attained to a high level of spirituality. It was a matter of selecting a qualified person and then issuing a call to serve, followed by an assignment to a particular job or position. The pattern was a familiar one, doing things in heaven as they would someday be done on earth.

Also in his epistle to the Ephesians, Paul said essentially the same thing. He told the people,

> Blessed be the God and Father of our Lord Jesus Christ, who hath blessed us with all spiritual blessings in heavenly places in Christ: according as he hath chosen us in him before the foundation of the world, that we should be holy and without blame before him in love:

> Having predestinated us unto the adoption of children by Jesus Christ to himself, according to the good pleasure of his will, to the praise of the glory of his grace, wherein he hath made us accepted in the beloved.[12]

In summary, this means that in the premortal life before the foundation of the world, there was that part of heaven which was designated as the elect, a group that had more successfully kept their first estate and were entitled to preferential status as they prepared for life experience on earth. They were the ones especially upon whom God would depend to implement and carry out heaven's plan. Another part, which was undoubtedly the large majority, would also be involved, depending on how they used their agency and what kind of potential they had developed.

Some of this is speculation, of course, but one thing is clear, and that is that in the previous lifetime, there was definitely a preferred group, people who had gained a greater degree of spirituality and consequently were elected to be an important power and influence in the life ahead. These were the Israelites, some of whom would later be called by that name and designated specifically as *the children of Israel.*

Among this elite population must have been all or most of the righteous people who descended from Adam down to Noah and the time of the Great Flood. Others who came later included many who lived in the days of Abraham, Isaac and Jacob, and also those who followed Moses across the plains of the Sinai Peninsula, all being set apart as a chosen group and reminded from time to time that they were a special and peculiar people above all other nations on earth.

Finally, down through the centuries there were still others, especially during the latter days, everyone making a predetermined appearance until the time when the great plan of heaven was completed. People were born at different times and in different places and circumstances, each according to his or her worthiness, including foreordination and election.

And yet there was one thing they all had in common, one thing that separated them from everyone else and gave them a name. All of these people were part of a unique and unusual organization, for example, which had its origin far back in the premortal life. Each person possessed a certified membership of record. Indeed, all were citizens and charter members of the original House of Israel!

Transfer to Earth

When it came time for the spirit children of God to begin transferring to earth, the logistics involved must have been tremendous. In addition to the creation of the earth itself, there was the matter of populating it, sending people down according to a predetermined time and place. Everything had to be worked out carefully in advance, and the principle guide and index used in making the determinations appear to have been in connection with the House of Israel.

In the Bible there are only two main scriptures which refer specifically to this vast movement of people and the system of distribution, but they are enough to give at least a general picture of what happened. One of them is found in a statement by Moses in the Book of Deuteronomy.

On one occasion he remarked,

Remember the days of old, consider the years of many generations: ask thy father, and he will shew thee; thy elders, and they will tell thee.

When the most High divided to the nations their inheritance, when he separated the sons of Adam, he set the bounds of the people according to the number of the children of Israel.

For the Lord's portion is his people; Jacob is the lot of his inheritance.[13]

In other words, the positioning of earth's inhabitants as to time and place was in direct relationship to Israelite influence in premortal life. The latter definitely appears to have been a controlling and determining factor. The result was that in the antediluvian period of world history, ending with the days of Noah, a patriarchal line of righteous men and women and their descendants stretched like a long spinal cord down through history, introducing mankind to a new environment and setting a pattern for the general distribution and alignment of people.

Also following the Great Flood, this same pattern continued, always with the idea that those in the House of Israel were an important group and would be given preferential treatment as to where and when people were born.

Another way of saying this is to paraphrase the statement by Moses, changing some of the original wording and adding an additional phrase: "When the most High divided to the nations their inheritance," for example, "when he separated the sons of Adam, *he established the lineages* and set the bounds of the people according to *whether or not they were members of the House of Israel.*"

The key phrase in this particular rewording, of course, is the one occurring at the very end. In the actual verse with no paraphrasing, which is from the King James Version of the Bible, the text states that God set the bounds of the people according to the number of the children of Israel. Certainly the significance of this type of statement, assuming it is correct, cannot be overstated as far as an Israelite connection is concerned. But at the same time there have also been other suggested meanings such as those found in different biblical translations.

In the New English Bible, to cite an example, the scripture in question states that the most High set the bounds of the people "according to the number of the sons of God," whereas in another example, the Greek translation of the Old Testament, it reads "according to the number of the angels of God."[14]

In relation to the principles of foreordination and election, however, the meaning found in the King James Version, as well as in certain other translations, could well be the most logical and correct.

Moreover, in addition to the scripture by Moses, there is a second one in the Bible which refers to the transfer of people from premortal life to earth, although without mentioning the children of Israel. It is contained in another statement given by the Apostle Paul. While speaking to a group of Athenians who were assembled on Mars Hill, he commented on a certain inscription that referred to an unknown God and told the people that it was this same being who had created the world and given life and breath to all things.

He then explained that it was also God who "hath made of one blood all nations of men for to dwell on all the face of the earth, and hath determined the times before appointed, and the bounds of their habitation."[15]

Along with the statement by Moses, therefore, this second one by Paul substantiates the idea that earth's inhabitants are all born at a predetermined time and place. Also the additional information given in the Book of Deuteronomy is that the placement of people in their respective times and places is coordinated in some way with that of the children of Israel, those who were members of the House of Israel in premortal life.

Theoretically, this means that the birth of all non-Israelites, both before and after the Flood and continuing down to the present time, has occurred chronologically and geographically in relation to the birth of those who are of the children of Israel. According to a very complex logistical plan, all forms of society have essentially been established in this way.

The concept, once again, is one of foreordination and election. It reaffirms that there was an agreement made in heaven in which the children of Israel were to be regarded preferentially and would receive an inheritance on earth that would benefit them both temporally and spiritually. Historically there might be exceptions, but in general it is those who are Israelites that are placed in the more favorable situations, those which would allow them to be a positive and determining influence among the nations and kingdoms of the world.

A Matter of Lineage

As people began populating the earth, it became obvious that even when a person was born under ideal circumstances, it was no assurance that he or she would lead a good life. The prime example, of course, was Cain who was among the first sons and daughters of Adam and Eve.

Since Cain turned out to be such a bad individual, even a son of perdition, it seems unlikely that he was of the House of Israel to begin with, despite the fact that he was born in a favorable time and place and in a good family lineage. In actuality, it appears that he set the precedent, showing there would be exceptions to the policy that those born as Israelites would be treated preferentially upon the earth.

Certainly there were other instances down through history besides Cain where people who were not of Israel, for one reason or another, might have been placed in an Israelite lineage. The two sons of Eber, for example, in the fifth generation after Noah and the Flood, represented two very different groups of people, Peleg following the way of his father and perpetuating the patriarchal line, and Joktan migrating to a new location and becoming the progenitor of an important Arab nation.

A second example occurred several generations later when the prophet Abraham had a son named Ishmael, who was the first member of the lineage known as the *seed of Abraham*. Under different circumstances he might have occupied a prestigious position, one with a birthright, but Ishmael had not been chosen and called ahead of time and therefore was not destined to be born into the designated line. Instead it was Isaac, the second son by a different marriage, who had been elected to this calling. He eventually became a great patriarch, whereas Ishmael went in a different direction and originated another branch of the Arabic people.

Although Isaac and Ishmael were both of the seed of

Abraham, it was only Isaac and certain of his descendants who were that part of the seed regarded as the covenant people, also referred to as *children of the promise.* They were those of the House of Israel who had been foreordained and called in the premortal life and were now continuing the same organization on earth.

In addition to these examples there were still others, among whom were Jacob and Esau, the two sons of Isaac. These were the famous twin brothers, born and raised in an elite Israelite family but with very different roles and callings. One became the father of twelve sons and the progenitor of the House of Israel, and the other, the ancestor of the people known in the Bible as Edomites.

It could well be, therefore, that Esau, like Joktan and Ishmael before him, never did belong to the House of Israel, and because of this his status on earth was far below that of his brother. Consequently, throughout biblical history, the Israelites and Edomites were often in conflict with one another, just as Jacob and Esau had been during their earlier lifetime, and to some extent even before coming from their mother's womb.

In conclusion, the Apostle Paul himself hinted strongly at one time that some of those of Israelite lineage were not just unrighteous Israelites, but actually were not members of the original House of Israel. "For they are not all Israel, which are of Israel," he said in his epistle to the Romans. "Neither, because they are the seed of Abraham are they all children," meaning *children of the promise.*[16]

In support of this idea, some of the Jewish people living in and around Jerusalem during the time of Christ also might be cited. Their disbelief and rebelliousness would suggest more than just a failure to live up to an Israelite heritage and background. Instead, they might have been Israelites by birth only and never had anything to do with the original House of Israel! On one occasion Jesus told the people,

> I know that ye are Abraham's seed, but ye seek to kill me, because my word hath no place in you.

And then he gave them the full truth.

If ye were Abraham's children, ye would do the works of Abraham.

Ye are of your father the devil, and the lusts of your father ye will do.

He that is of God heareth God's words: ye therefore hear them not, because ye are not of God.[17]

There were times when Jesus stated outright that some of the people were prepared to hear his message and others were not. In answer to some of their questions, for example, he replied, "I am the good shepherd, and know my sheep, and am known of mine. My sheep hear my voice, and I know them, and they follow me."

He also made it clear that it was his Father in heaven who had actually given certain people to him. "My Father, which gave them me, is greater than all," he said, "and no man is able to pluck them out of my Father's hand. All that the Father giveth me shall come to me; and him that cometh to me I will in no wise cast out."[18]

What this suggests, once again, is that the logistical process of transferring people to earth from premortal life was very intricate and complex. It was not just a matter of always placing Israelites in one kind of situation and non-Israelites in another, but there was evidently a certain amount of mixing involved.

In other words, in the administration of heaven's plan, people such as Cain, Joktan, Ishmael and Esau were introduced at times when, in connection with their agency and inclination, they would be able to fulfill particular roles. It was not that they were foreordained to do this, but rather put in a position where they could do what the Lord knew in advance that they would do.

Of course, the most glaring example in all of this, and the one that is most ironic, is the rebellious Jews in Jerusalem, the ones who by birth were of the seed of Abraham and supposedly also the children of promise. They were those who were situated in the exact time and place where, after several thousand years of world history, they could finally receive and accept the Messiah. They were the only ones among all of the Israelites who were to have such an opportunity.

And yet for whatever reasons, which for so long have been their nemesis and condemnation, they crucified him, the one who was not only the Messiah and the Son of God but in actuality the creator of the earth and the ruling head of the House of Israel!

Son of the Morning

The idea that some of the people in premortal life who were not Israelites were nevertheless born into a preferred lineage on earth helps to explain certain events which happened down through history, the most noticeable once again being Christ's rejection by the Jews. Those who adamantly approved of his crucifixion might well have had no inclination against it because they had no Israelite background, and had they been members of the original House of Israel, they possibly would have acted much differently.

And yet the other possibility obviously exists, and that is that people like the disbelieving Jews had actually been Israelites in their previous lifetime yet following the transfer to earth had misused their agency and failed to carry out heaven's plan!

The risk of failure, in fact, is always an inherent part of the principle of agency and the right to choose. From the beginning, there was no guarantee that life on earth would be successful. The important thing was for people to be tested under new conditions to see in which direction they would go, but the chance for failure was always there, just as it had been in the premortal life.

During the war in heaven, for example, when Michael and his angels fought against those who followed Satan, billions of people had to make a choice. It was a dramatic turning point and a giant crossroad of decision. There were undoubtedly many discussions and exchanges of opinion, with both sides holding to their view, but in the end many found themselves on the wrong side and consequently were cast out of heaven and banished forever.

It was one of those instances where people who had once been obedient and faithful finally allowed themselves to be swayed to an errant viewpoint by a persuasive leader with a new idea.

In those days, Satan was known as Lucifer, a *son of the morning,* and one of the leading angels and bright stars of heaven. He had risen to a very high standing, evidently within the House of Israel itself, and was a person of considerable authority in the presence of God. But his controversial ideas, especially in regard to agency, were contrary to the plan of deity, and in process of time he rebelled, taking a third part of heaven with him.

In the Book of Revelation in the New Testament, John spoke of this event, referring to Lucifer or Satan as the dragon. "And there appeared another wonder in heaven," he said, "and behold a great red dragon, having seven heads and ten horns, and seven crowns upon his heads. And his tail drew the third part of the stars of heaven, and did cast them to the earth."

> And there was war in heaven: Michael and his angels fought against the dragon; and the dragon fought and his angels, and prevailed not; neither was their place found anymore in heaven. And the great dragon was cast out, that old serpent, called the Devil, and Satan, which deceiveth the whole world: he was cast out into the earth, and his angels were cast out with him.[19]

At the time that Lucifer fell, it is said that the heavens wept over him, knowing that he was once an important person but was now lost forever. Because he disagreed with God, and even tried to assume some of his power and authority, he and those with him lost any chance they might have had for future progression.

In connection with this event, the prophet Isaiah had Lucifer in mind on one occasion when he referred to the King of Babylon, making the king the namesake of his notorious predecessor and comparing one with the other.

> How art thou fallen from heaven, O Lucifer, son of the morning! How art thou cut down to the ground, which didst weaken the nations!

For thou hast said in thine heart, I will ascend into heaven, I will exalt my throne above the stars of God: I will sit also upon the mount of the congregation, in the sides of the north: I will ascend above the heights of the clouds; I will be like the most High. Yet thou shalt be brought down to hell, to the sides of the pit.[20]

As a result of his rebellion, therefore, Lucifer became the grand prototype in history of someone who once had been of high standing but later failed. He represents anyone who might be in a position where he can benefit not only himself but others, and yet elects not to do so. And because of this, he established a potential, as it were, for others in the future to do the same thing, to progress to a place of great importance and then lose it by making the wrong decisions and choices.

The possibility of failure during life experience, in other words, would always be there. It was included in heaven's plan from the beginning and would definitely continue to be a part of freedom of choice and agency during the coming lifetime on earth.

Part Two

The House of Israel on Earth

A New Beginning

As Moses led the Israelite captives out of Egypt, following their long period of bondage, he told them how the Lord had established the lineages on earth and set the policy for distributing the people.

> When the most High divided to the nations their inheritance, when he separated the sons of Adam, he set the bounds of the people according to the number of the children of Israel.[21]

Centuries later the Apostle Paul alluded to this same situation.

Beginning with the time of Adam, those transferring to earth from premortal life were positioned in time and place according to whether or not they belonged to the original House of Israel. By way of previous agreement, Israelites were generally placed in the more favorable geographical areas and under better conditions. The patriarchal line especially, along with its righteous descendants, was in this category and formed a major part of the advance group of people.

It did not take long for dissensions to occur, however, and by the time of the seventh generation there was already a large division of society, those on one side who had followed the way of the patriarchs and on the other the wayward posterity of Adam, including many who were descendants of Cain. Certainly it was an implication that Israelites were now being born on the one hand and non-Israelites on the other, although again there is always the possibility that some of those who appeared to be in the latter group were actually part of heaven's elect who had failed to accomplish their purpose in life through a misuse of agency.

Consequently, at this point in history after the first seven generations, two figures stand out as being representative of the particular group people had chosen to follow. In the group comprising the patriarchs was Enoch, one of those in the patriarchal line who became a great prophet and leader among his people. In the other was Lamech, a descendant of Cain and one mentioned specifically in the Bible as someone who followed in the tradition of his errant predecessor. These two especially were symbolic of how mankind was faring upon the earth.

And then after that, it was only four more generations before all of earth's inhabitants except eight were swept away by a giant flood. Prior to that time, Enoch and the righteous part of society had either died or been taken from the earth, making way for the demise of everyone who had gone astray and were in opposition to heaven's plan. It was undoubtedly the world's greatest natural disaster and suggests that many or most of those involved, because of their degenerate condition, were never of the House of Israel in the first place.

Finally, in the aftermath of the Great Flood, everything started anew. The patriarchal line continued, and the different lineages were again put into operation. Man's lifetime became noticeably shorter, and eleven more generations came into being, bringing the time in history down to the days of the three great patriarchs: Abraham, Isaac and Jacob, the men whose names have so often been associated with the House of Israel, as well as with the name of deity itself.

It was Abraham, in fact, who initiated the famous genealogical line known in the Bible as the *seed of Abraham,* following which the House of Israel, as a formal institution and kingdom upon the earth, was officially organized and brought into being by his grandson Jacob.

An Illustrious Family

At the time that Jacob was born, he was preceded in birth by his twin brother Esau who consequently inherited the position of birthright. But Esau evidently never considered such a thing to be very important, and according to the well-known incident recorded in the Bible, he sold the birthright to Jacob for some bread and pottage. Later when it came time to receive a special blessing from his father, Esau lost that to Jacob also, due to some clever trickery by their mother, and following which he immediately started making plans for revenge.

Recognizing the seriousness of the situation, therefore, and heeding the advice of his parents, Jacob decided to leave Palestine for a while and travel northward into Mesopotamia, not just to escape a death threat from Esau but for another reason as well, that of finding a wife among some of his relatives and starting a family.

Surely on that occasion he must have sensed some kind of turning point in his life, and also a presentiment that important things were in store for him. This became evident soon after his departure when he had an unusual dream one night at a place that he later called Bethel. On a stairway leading to heaven, he saw angels ascending and descending, and at the top was the Lord himself who spoke to him, giving him the same blessings and promises which earlier had been given to Isaac and Abraham. Among these was the statement that through him and his posterity, all nations of the earth would be blessed.

It was undoubtedly a blessing he was already familiar with, having heard it from his father and grandfather before him, but now that he received the same promises for himself, he must have known that he, along with them, had been foreordained to a very important calling.

Years later, when he was returning to Palestine from Mesopotamia, he again stopped at Bethel where the Lord gave him the same covenant blessings. In addition, he officially gave Jacob a new name.

> Thy name is Jacob: thy name shall not be called anymore Jacob, but Israel shall be thy name: and he called his name Israel.[22]

In this way the name of Israel first came into existence, except for a brief mention of it earlier by an angel. The name was one that would be magnified in many ways and would become a watchword and symbol for centuries to come. Indeed, it was the name that served as a connecting link between premortal life and the hereafter. And as far as life on earth was concerned, it was the one specific reference which applied not only to Jacob, but also to his illustrious family who came into being during the productive years that he spent in Mesopotamia.

It was in those earlier years, for example, that he married two of his cousins, and also their two handmaidens, by whom he had eleven sons and a daughter. One other son was born on his return trip to Palestine, bringing the number of male members to the historic figure of twelve. All together they constituted the family of Jacob, each of the sons eventually becoming the head of a tribe and known collectively in biblical history as the twelve sons and tribes of Israel.

These were the men who apparently had been foreordained and elected in premortal life to be the twelve progenitors of the House of Israel on earth. They were the ones who had been designated as the vanguard of those who would now be regarded officially as Israelites. These men were the original charter members, so to speak, the twelve patriarchs at the head of their tribes and also the founding fathers.

And yet in so many ways, it was a very unauspicious beginning. From the outset, it became obvious that the older sons especially were not that faithful or obedient. Reuben had an affair with one of his father's concubines, Simeon and Levi instigated a massacre in a neighboring town, and Judah married into a Canaanite family and inadvertently became the father of his daughter-in-law's child. Then it was all of the sons together, except Reuben and Benjamin, who later planned the death and exile of their younger brother Joseph and were the ones responsible for him being sold into Egypt.

This last event got the House of Israel off to a shaky start. What happened was not only a criminal act, casting an unfavorable light on an undisciplined group of brothers, but foreshadowed many instances that would occur in the future— a long series of events showing the errant ways and human weaknesses of mankind that someday would split the House of Israel in two and eventually scatter it to many different parts of the world.

Ascendancy of Ephraim

The story of Joseph, the brother who began a career in Egypt as a slave and then rose to a position of great power, is well documented in the Bible. As a person of high standing whose position was second only to that of Pharaoh, he was a ruler over all of Egypt and eventually brought his entire family out of Palestine during a time of famine and gave them property next to him in the land of Goshen.

In the meantime, he married a girl named Asenath, a daughter of Potipherah, the Priest of On. Since her father was also referred to as a prince, she in turn might be regarded as a princess with considerable royal standing. It was Pharaoh himself, in fact, who had arranged their marriage in the first place.

To Joseph and Asenath were born two sons, Manasseh and Ephraim, two young princes with Israelite ancestry who together were raised in a royal Egyptian household. Manasseh was the elder and consequently possessed the birthright, yet it was Ephraim who eventually was preferred before him and thus inherited a more important blessing.

Ephraim at that time was growing up with an Egyptian peer group and possibly was unaware of any kind of Israelite inheritance. Actually, he might have had little to do at all with the people coming in from Palestine. But his heritage was Israelite as well as Egyptian, and according to an apparent foreordination which had taken place in premortal life, he soon would occupy a highly important position, at least theoretically, within the leadership of the new House of Israel.

It is unknown why Ephraim was singled out from all of those around him and given a special type of recognition. But that is exactly what happened, and it took place according to three main steps.

First, there was the occasion on which he gained preference

28

over his brother Manasseh, even though it was the latter who supposedly had the birthright. This occurred when the two boys went with their father one day to visit Jacob who was very old and about to die. When their grandfather offered to give them a blessing, Joseph placed his sons in such a way that Jacob's right hand would be in front of Manasseh and his left in front of Ephraim, making it so his older son would be in a position to receive the main blessing. But Jacob, "guiding his hands wittingly," crossed them over so that his right hand rested upon the head of Ephraim.

Joseph knew that his father had poor vision and could hardly see because of age, so he reached forth his own hand trying to correct him. "Not so, my father," he said, pointing toward Manasseh, "for this is the firstborn; put they right hand upon his head."

But his father refused and said,

> I know it, my son, I know it: he also shall become a people, and he also shall be great: but truly his younger brother shall be greater than he, and his seed shall become a multitude of nations.[23]

Jacob blessed both grandsons that day, each with his own promises and each in the proper order. Each was given a promise of greatness and also the assurance that his posterity would be numerous. But it was Ephraim who received the greater blessing, the reason for which was unknown to Joseph at the time, and possibly even to some degree to his father Jacob. And yet the purpose of it all had been arranged much earlier during a former time period when many such matters were worked out in advance.

This was evident in the second step, for example, in which Ephraim gained special recognition, a process that involved Reuben, his father's oldest brother. Because Reuben was the firstborn in his family, he started out with the family birthright, like Esau before him had done, but due to certain circumstances he lost it, and consequently it was given to someone else.

In this case the loss was the result of an affair which Reuben had with Bilhah, one of Jacob's concubines. The incident occurred sometime after the family had come from Mesopotamia to Palestine, and according to the account recorded in the Bible, it was the main reason for Reuben losing his birthright. What happened, however, was likely related more to an earlier foreordination and election than to any earthly circumstances.

As things turned out, the birthright in question ended up jointly with both Ephraim and Manasseh. In connection with this event, the biblical record states that it was Reuben who was the firstborn, "but foreasmuch as he defiled his father's bed, his birthright was given unto the sons of Joseph, the son of Israel." [24]

All of this was preliminary, therefore, to the third and final step in which Ephraim ascended to a high position of authority, one where he alone acquired the main part of the Israelite birthright. Documentation for such is extremely brief, but it does exist in a single statement made by the prophet Jeremiah as recorded in the Bible. "I am a father to Israel," he said at one time, speaking for the Lord, "and Ephraim is my firstborn." [25]

Of course, it might be argued that such a small scriptural reference is not enough to confirm the authority of Ephraim over Manasseh, and that the birthright continued to be shared equally by the two brothers together. And were it not for the unusual blessing given earlier by Jacob, this kind of statement might be reasonable.

But the implication and evidence definitely exist that not only did Ephraim obtain the birthright and gain seniority over his older brother, but he was also the one who had been called and elected in premortal life to be the leading individual in Israelite affairs. He was the one specifically designated to fill this strategic role. His posterity was to form a genealogical line that would extend far into the future, exerting a strong influence on all of the other tribes and eventually in the latter days, prior to the thousand years known as the Millennium, become the main force of leadership within the entire House of Israel!

The Shadow of Joseph

Despite the prominence of Ephraim in his position of holding the birthright, as well as being the House of Israel's firstborn, it was actually his father Joseph who was the shadow and true source of his authority. In a real sense, it was Joseph who inherited the birthright at the time he became the savior of his family by bringing them from the land of Palestine into Egypt. On one occasion he told them,

> Now therefore be not grieved, nor angry with yourselves, that ye sold me hither: for God did send me before you to preserve life.

> And God sent me before you to preserve you a posterity in the earth, and to save your lives by a great deliverance.[26]

Certainly if there was anyone who had received a previous foreordination and election, it was Joseph. His life and mission on earth implied that he had been called and chosen to accomplish all that was ascribed to him. And as things turned out, he was one of the four main forerunners in Israelite history, along with Abraham, Isaac and Jacob.

By name, Joseph never did become the head of one of the twelve tribes, and yet he was doubly represented by his two sons, each of whom occupied that position. Levi was another who was not counted among the original group, in his case because of religious responsibilities. The resulting twelve tribes of Israel, therefore, which became so well known down through history, comprised those who descended from ten of Israel's sons plus two of his grandsons, Ephraim and Manasseh.

It was also Joseph who received a distinguished patriarchal blessing from his father just before the latter's death. Both he and his brother Judah were given promises on that occasion which were far superior to those of the other sons, although Joseph's blessing suggested that his posterity through Ephraim

31

and Manasseh would have a more promising future.

As far as his two sons were concerned, however, it is probable that neither one of them ever got too involved in Israelite affairs. Being partly under the influence of their mother, and Joseph being occupied with matters of state, their upbringing was very likely mainly Egyptian.

At the time of the unique blessings given by their grandfather Jacob, the two boys would have been in their early or mid-twenties, fully capable of understanding the words spoken if they were familiar with the language, yet because of their connection with Egyptian culture once again, they might have been unaware of what was actually going on. Even Joseph undoubtedly had questions.

But there was one thing now that Joseph could definitely be sure of, and that was that the posterity of his two sons would be numerous and great, and that one of them especially, the one he had named Ephraim and whose name signified fruitful, would be involved in a very unusual destiny.

Foundation of a House

During the time of famine when Jacob responded to Joseph's call and brought his family out of Palestine, the group numbered sixty-six people, according to the Bible, plus all of the wives. In addition, there were Joseph and his wife and their two sons, who were in Egypt to begin with, which means that the initial members of the House of Israel were probably close to eighty-five in number. Only two daughters are mentioned in the biblical record, however, so a more accurate count of people might still be higher.

It was after that, of course, that the children of Israel spent the next 430 years in the lower part of Egypt, most of the time as slaves, where they multiplied into a large nation. Some accounts say that the period of time was only half that long, but in any case, when it finally ended and many new generations had arisen, it might have been well over two million men, women and children who left Egyptian soil under the leadership of Moses and Aaron and began the long trek to Palestine.

> And the children of Israel journeyed from Rameses to Succoth, about six hundred thousand on foot that were men, beside children. And a mixed multitude went with them; and flocks, and herds, even very much cattle.[27]

Then sometime later, during their second year of travel, the first official census was taken among the House of Israel's population. On the first day of the second month, in the wilderness of Sinai, the Lord commanded Moses and Aaron to conduct a poll of all male members twenty years old and upward who were able to go to war. No others, including women and children, were numbered, and the final count was 603,550. From this number once again, an estimate of total population might possibly have been between two and three million people!

At the same time, however, it is also possible that there were errors in the translation and transcription of the Bible, which consequently might have produced population figures that were distorted or too high. A surprising and much more conservative estimate of the number of Israelites coming out of Egypt has been as low as 72,000.

Yet the biblical record as it now stands has to be considered carefully. First, there is the matter of the long period of time that the Israelites were in captivity, whether 430 years or half that amount. This provided ample opportunity to develop a huge population. Second, there is the serious threat that Israelite captives eventually posed to the Egyptian government, which again suggests a large number of people.

> And the children of Israel were fruitful, and increased abundantly, and multiplied, and waxed exceeding mighty; and the land was filled with them.
>
> And he (the Pharaoh) said unto his people, Behold, the people of the children of Israel are more and mightier than we:
>
> Come on, let us deal wisely with them; lest they multiply, and it come to pass that when there falleth out any war, they join also unto our enemies, and fight against us.
>
> Therefore, they did set over them taskmasters to afflict them with their burdens.
>
> But the more they afflicted them, the more they multiplied and grew. And they were grieved because of the children of Israel.[28]

Concerning the descendants of Ephraim and Manasseh at this time, as to how much they were involved in the captivity and to what extent their Egyptian ancestry might have provided any kind of preference or immunity, the account in the Bible is silent. Their particular circumstances and family ties which they had with Potipherah, the Priest of On, might or might not have made a difference.

One thing is certain, however, and that is that when it came time for the children of Israel to begin their long trek across the desert, the tribes of Ephraim and Manasseh were both present and formed an important part of the migration. Their numbers were generally smaller than the other tribes, yet when joined together as the posterity of Joseph, they were by far the largest group except for Judah.

According to the census figures taken in the wilderness of Sinai, the tribe of Judah numbered 74,600 men who were 20 years old and upward and able to go war. The tribes of Ephraim and Manasseh, on the other hand, were 40,500 and 32,200 respectively, forming a total of 72,700. Certainly these were impressive numbers, and along with all of the other tribes together, they constituted not only a major threat to the Egyptian pharaoh and his government but were the underlying foundation for the rapidly growing population of the House of Israel.

The Wilderness of Sinai

The itinerary of Israelite travel from Egypt to the promised land in Palestine was long and varied, stretching for hundreds of miles across the Sinai peninsula and covering a time period of more than forty years. It was a journey filled with almost unbelievable events and circumstances and was the process by which the children of Israel made the difficult transition from slavery to independence and became a significant nation in the Middle East.

And among all of their stopping points along the way, the most important by far was one which they reached only a couple of months after leaving Egypt, a desert area referred to in the Bible as the wilderness of Sinai. At this location, where Moses had once kept the flock of his father-in-law Jethro and where he had seen the mysterious burning bush, the people established a camp that was to be their home for almost a year.

It was here that the Lord gave the Israelites ten commandments written upon tables of stone and also provided them with detailed instructions on how to build and furnish a tabernacle. In addition, it was the place where Moses and Aaron would soon conduct the first census of the House of Israel.

Indeed, this was the place where God made several important appearances before Moses and his vast congregation. Never before had spiritual manifestations of such great magnitude taken place in the presence of so many people. With Mount Sinai looming in the background and possibly two to three million people camped in the desert below, it was an impressive setting for some of the most significant events recorded in the Bible.

And an important part in all of this was the children of Israel themselves, the people who belonged to the House by the same name and who were now assembled in the wilderness of Sinai as migrating tribes. These were the progeny of Jacob and his twelve sons whose prestigious ancestors were Isaac and also the great patriarch Abraham.

In actuality, Abraham's first son had been a man named Ishmael, one who might have had a legal birthright yet had not received the necessary blessing. Consequently, he started on a different course in life, probably not having been an Israelite in the premortal life to begin with and thus being foreordained to a different lineage and geographic location on earth.

Prior to his birth, the Lord said,

> Behold, I have blessed him, and will make him fruitful, and will multiply him exceedingly; twelve princes shall he beget, and I will make him a great nation.

Each of Ishmael's twelve sons became the head of a tribe and together were the progenitors of an important branch of the Arabic people. They are listed by name in the Bible, "by their towns, and by their castles; twelve princes according to their nations."[29] And yet for reasons unknown and yet implied, they were not those of the chosen line.

Instead, it was the twelve sons of Jacob who now were at the forefront and whose posterity would someday be a leading force in the affairs of mankind. They were the ones who had initiated the earthly organization known as the House of Israel, a society that would become as numerous as the stars in heaven and the sand upon the seashore, and through which all nations of the earth would be blessed. Along with the righteous Israelites in the centuries before them, they were those who had been called and elected to lead the way on earth in promoting a religious lifestyle and carrying out heaven's plan.

And in the midst of all of this, it was now that the children of Israel came out of a long period of Egyptian bondage and began their historic journey across the desert. In the wilderness of Sinai, at the site of a famous mountain, they received important laws and commandments and were officially set apart by the hand of God. Then under the leadership of Moses and his brother Aaron, they organized themselves into twelve tribes and entered a new and eventful period of Israelite history, one that would eventually take them in every direction and into many different parts of the earth!

A Number of Twelve

Before Moses received the ten commandments on stone tablets, he was first given them verbally by the Lord, along with certain other laws and ordinances. These he recorded in what was called the *book of the covenant* which he prepared to read before the people.

Prior to doing this, however, he arose early in the morning and built an altar under a hill on which to offer sacrifices. He then did something very unusual, although not wholly unprecedented. In the vicinity of the altar he erected twelve pillars, each one representing one of the twelve tribes of Israel.

It was similar to something Jacob had done many years earlier when on two different occasions he visited the place known as Bethel. On a spot which he referred to as the *house of God*, he set up a pillar of stone and then poured oil upon it. It was symbolic of something very important to Jacob, as well as a memorial to a particular event and a reminder of what had happened.

In connection with the twelve pillars erected by Moses, there was also a special significance in regard to the number of twelve itself. Especially in Israelite history, this particular number was used again and again to refer either specifically or indirectly to the existence of the twelve tribes. It became a trademark, as it were, and an identifying distinction and characteristic.

One instance of this was in the preparation of the *breast-plate of judgment*, part of the clothing and equipment pertaining to the tabernacle of the congregation, a large structure soon to be built in the Sinai desert. It was a packet containing an instrument known as the Urim and Thummim and would be worn in front of Aaron's outer garment when he officiated in the priestly office.

On the face of the breastplate were attached twelve gems or precious stones. These had been donated by certain rulers in

Israel and were cut and set by Bezaleel, the chief builder and engineer of the tabernacle and its furnishings.

> And he made the breastplate of cunning work, like the work of the ephod; of gold, blue, and purple, and scarlet, and fine twined linen.
>
> And they set in it four rows of stones: the first row was a sardius, a topaz, and a carbuncle: this was the first row.
>
> And the second row, an emerald, a sapphire, and a diamond. And the third row, a ligure, an agate, and an amethyst.
>
> And the fourth row, a beryl, an onyx, and a jasper: they were inclosed in ouches of gold in their inclosings.
>
> And the stones were according to the names of the children of Israel, twelve according to their names, like the engravings of a signet, every one with his name, according to the twelve tribes.[30]

Such a display of gems, against the bright colors of linen, made the breastplate an impressive article of clothing that was to be used by the high priest. Whenever Aaron went into the tabernacle with this sacred packet worn in front of him, it represented him bearing the names of the children of Israel upon his heart "for a memorial before the Lord continually." At the same time, it symbolized the heritage and fortunes of the Israelite nation which was now en route to a promised land.

Still another example of the number twelve was in relation to the office of *prince* within the organization of the House of Israel. Twelve men occupied this position, all of them select individuals and each one the renowned head and leader of a tribe.

The first mention of them, as noted in the Bible, was at the completion of the tabernacle which occurred on the first day of the second year after the Israelites had come out of Egypt. On that occasion, Moses anointed and sanctified the sacred structure, including the large tent and all of the different furnishings and equipment, after which the twelve princes brought forth their offerings for the dedication of the altar. This they accomplished by using six covered wagons, each pulled by a pair of oxen.

On twelve consecutive days, the princes took turns in appearing before the sacred altar. Beginning with the tribe of Judah and ending with Naphtali, their offerings were identical, consisting of one silver charger and a silver bowl, both of them filled with fine flour mingled with oil, and also a golden spoon full of incense. After that came the animals to be sacrificed: one bullock, one ram, six lambs of the first year, one kid of the goats, two oxen, five rams, and five goats.

When all of this was completed, Moses concluded the ceremony by going into the innermost part of the tabernacle known as the Holy of Holies. Here as he had done earlier at the burning bush and on Mount Sinai he spoke personally with the Lord. Certainly it was a momentous occasion, an important milestone during the trek from Egypt and one that helped prepare the people spiritually for the difficult years that lay ahead.

Eve of Departure

Nineteen days before the children of Israel resumed their journey toward the promised land, the Lord once more spoke with Moses in the wilderness of Sinai. "Take ye the sum of all the congregation of the children of Israel," he said, "after their families, by the house of their fathers, with the number of their names, every male by their polls; from twenty years old and upward, all that are able to go forth to war in Israel.

> Thou and Aaron shall number them by their armies. And with you there shall be a man of every tribe; every one head of the house of his fathers.

Again it was the twelve princes of Israel who officiated on this occasion, those who had dedicated the altar of the tabernacle and who in the future would be involved in other such ordinances and functions. They are listed by name and genealogy in the Book of Numbers in the Bible and "were the renowned of the congregation, princes of the tribes of their fathers, heads of thousands in Israel.[31]

Indeed, it was these men who were the main ecclesiastical figures under Moses and Aaron as far as the Israelites in general were concerned and were significant forerunners of the twelve apostles who lived in the time of Jesus. They were the distinguished and the elite in Israel, and aside from Moses himself they appear to have been the main source of leadership among the tribes.

In connection with the census count, for example, it was evidently the princes who provided the numbers for their particular tribes, the grand total being 603,550 males, age twenty years and older who were able to go to war. This again suggests the calculated figure of two to three million people for the combined population of the House of Israel, allowing for the possibility that figures listed in the Bible might sometimes be distorted or too high.

Following the census count, and as the Israelites prepared for a coming departure, the Lord once more spoke unto Moses, and also to Aaron, and told them to set up a camping plan. "Every man of the children of Israel shall pitch by his own standard," he told them, "with the ensign of their father's house: far off about the tabernacle of the congregation shall they pitch." He then gave them more detailed instructions.

To begin with, the plan was for the tribe of Levi to be camped immediately surrounding the newly-constructed tabernacle, with Moses and Aaron, along with Aaron's sons, situated directly in front of the entrance. Then to the east of the tabernacle was the camp of Judah, comprising the tribes of Judah, Issachar and Zebulun. To the south was the camp of Reuben, with the tribes of Reuben, Simeon and Gad. After these came the camp of Ephraim in the west, comprising the tribes of Ephraim, Manasseh and Benjamin. Finally was the camp of Dan in the north, with the tribes of Dan, Asher and Naphtali.

When the time arrived for the tribes to depart, the camp of Judah would go first and leading the way, followed by the Levites, who would transport the disassembled tabernacle. Then would come the camp of Reuben, after which other Levites would bring the sanctuary including the most holy things. Next would be the camps of Ephraim and Dan respectively at the back. Each tribe would be led by a prince, who also served as captain, with the implied places of honor in the march being those of Judah at the front and Ephraim directly behind the sanctuary of the tabernacle.[32]

In this manner, during the journey which lay ahead, the Israelites would move from place to place across the inhospitable deserts of the Sinai Peninsula. Destined to wander forty years because of discontent and rebelliousness, they would pass through a long series of camps after leaving Sinai, always according to a prescribed pattern of travel and following a large pillar of cloud by day and a pillar of fire by night that moved before them.

In the process of travel, it would be the princes of Judah and

Ephraim in the forefront. In their positions of honor in connection with the traveling tabernacle, they were the stalwarts among the twelve tribes and a primary source of leadership behind Moses and Aaron.

These were the men whose predecessors had received the notable blessings under the hand of Jacob. Above everyone else, they were the two who appeared to be the favored ones, those whose tribal forecasts for the future were more detailed and comprehensive than the others. Indeed, they were the very elite among their brethren. Unfortunately, it was also these particular tribes who someday would be in the midst of political confrontations within the House of Israel, those that would literally split it apart and eventually lead to its disintegration and downfall.

N 5th

Dan
Asher
Naphtali

go 1st

E Judah
Caleb
Issacher
Zebulun

W 4th Joshua
Ephraim
Menasseh
Benjamin

Moses
Aaron
Levi 2nd

S

3rd
Reuben
Simeon
Gad

Rebellion at Kadesh-Barnea

Soon after leaving the wilderness of Sinai, the Israelites arrived at a place called Kadesh-Barnea and from there sent out a reconnaissance group to explore Canaan, the future land of promise. The intent was to "spy out the land" and see what the future prospects were for entering the area. For this purpose, twelve men were selected, all important leaders within the twelve tribes.

> Get you up this way southward, and go up into the mountain:
>
> And see the land, what it is; and the people that dwelleth therein, whether they be strong or weak, few or many;
>
> And what the land is that they dwell in, whether it be good or bad; and what cities they be that they dwell in, whether in tents, or in strongholds;
>
> And what the land is, whether it be fat or lean, whether there be wood therein, or not. [33]

After forty days, however, when the men returned from their mission, an unfortunate event occurred which proved to be disastrous for most of the people within the Israelite congregation. All but two of the men in the search party gave a negative report of what they had seen, saying that the land was good but that the people and their walled cities were too strong and formidable to conquer. Some of the people were giants, they said, and made the Israelites look like grasshoppers.

Because of this report, the people were quick to rebel against Moses and Aaron, and they immediately started making plans to vacate camp and return to Egypt. Joshua and Caleb, those who had brought a more optimistic report from Canaan, tried to dissuade them, but the people refused to listen. Indeed, they would have stoned the two men had not the glory of the Lord suddenly appeared in the tabernacle of the congregation.

At that time the Lord delivered some shocking news to

Moses. Because of the rebelliousness of the people, he said, and all of their murmurings against him, none of those who had been part of the census taken at Sinai except Joshua and Caleb would ever see the promised land. During the next thirty-eight years, all were destined to die in the wilderness, and it was mainly their children who had not been numbered in the original census that would be permitted to enter Canaan.

Certainly it was a dire prediction and a devastating forecast, and yet necessary in the unfolding history of the House of Israel. It was just one more instance which showed the slow and gradual process by which a chosen people was developing into a strong society and nation. Although it was this same group who presumably had been among the most faithful in premortal life and had earned a preferred condition on earth, they still needed more time to grow and mature and also to raise up a new generation.

In the meantime, all plans for a return to Egypt were canceled, and the people commenced a long period of wandering in the wilderness. Under the continued leadership of Moses and Aaron, they traveled from place to place and from camp to camp across the deserts of the Sinai Peninsula, always taking with them the sacred tabernacle and following the pillars of cloud and fire.

And as they did so, it became increasingly apparent that times were changing and that others were now coming to the forefront in the leadership of the House of Israel. Joshua especially, a member of the tribe of Ephraim and one who had been with Moses on Mount Sinai, was gradually making his way to the top and would one day take the place of Moses himself. It would be under his leadership, in fact, that the children of Israel would finally enter the promised land.

He and Caleb would both play important roles in the future invasion of Canaan. Representing the tribes of Ephraim and Judah respectively, the two men who had stood out from the beginning would now provide the main source of responsibility and leadership.

Joshua would be the commanding general of the invading forces, and Caleb would be the one to deal with the children of Anak, the giants whom the Israelites feared so much and who had caused them to rebel against Moses. Out of more than 600,000 men who had been numbered in the census at Sinai, only Joshua and Caleb would actually be involved in the coming conquest of Canaan.

It was a natural consequence, therefore, that the two sons of Jacob who had received the most important blessings from their father long ago were now the ones whose tribes were in the important positions of Israelite leadership. It was also no surprise that Joshua and Caleb were the only two men who brought back a favorable report from Canaan, as well as the only ones who gave support to Moses and Aaron.

And in the future it would be no different. Ephraim and Judah would continue to be in leading positions in the House of Israel which was now preparing to enter a grand new phase of its history.

The Plains of Moab

The last stop on the Israelite's long itinerary of travel in the wilderness was the plains of Moab near Jericho. It was here that three major events took place prior to the children of Israel entering the promised land.

The first of these events was a second census conducted by Moses and Eleazar, the son of Aaron, prior to a division and distribution of land among the twelve tribes east of the Jordan River and in the land of Canaan. The poll taken provided not only a count of the population but also revealed a very significant fact: the number of people at the end of the long journey from Egypt was now less than it had been at the beginning!

After forty years in the wilderness the number of males twenty years and older who were eligible for war was 601,730, compared to the first census total of 603,550. Certainly it was apparent from the outset that plagues, sickness, and acts of retribution had all taken their toll.

Had it not been for the lack of faith and obedience among the people, the population prior to entering the promised land would have been much higher. And yet things did not turn out that way. Also because the so-called children of promise had murmured over economic conditions or turned to idolatry in their religious practices, they forfeited many of the rewards which otherwise they might have had.

Moses told the people who remained,

Understand therefore, that the Lord thy God giveth thee not this good land to possess it for thy righteousness; for thou art a stiffnecked people.

Remember, and forget not, how thou provokedst the Lord thy God to wrath in the wilderness: from the day that thou didst depart out of the land of Egypt, until ye came unto this place, ye have been rebellious against the Lord.[34]

It was a stark reminder to the people of their inconsistency and unfaithfulness. Through no particular merit of their own were they receiving an inheritance. It was strictly an act of benevolence from the Lord, a time when previous transgressions were set aside and a new opportunity placed before them.

In addition to the census count, which numbered the people in the House of Israel, this was also a time when men were selected to divide the land of Canaan among ten of the tribes. Reuben and Gad and part of the tribe of Manasseh had already been promised specific inheritances east of the Jordan River, but the rest were now to receive allotments in the large area of territory to the west.

The division and distribution of land were to be supervised by Joshua and Eleazar the priest, with one prince from each of the ten tribes assisting. Everything would basically be done according to lot. It was a significant undertaking, one that signaled not only the beginning of a new era of Israelite history but also the approach of a long military campaign. Along with the allotments of territory, there would inevitably come the tedious process of invading and conquering it.

One final important event took place on the plains of Moab after the census was taken and an organization set up for distributing the land. It occurred at a time when Moses had grown old and was about to leave his people. He himself would not enter the land of promise, but before the others did, he wanted to be sure they were ready. And so he gave them his final counsel and instructions, later recorded in the Book of Deuteronomy, and among these were certain predictions and forecasts for the future, patriarchal blessings, as it were, bestowed upon each of the twelve tribes of Israel.

Patriarchal Blessings

The tribal blessings given by Moses on the plains of Moab were a sequel to those that had been given by Jacob shortly before his death. During that former time period, the aged patriarch sent a message to his twelve sons, all of whom except Joseph had come into Egypt seventeen years earlier.

> Gather yourselves together, that I may tell you that which shall befall you in the last days. Gather yourselves together, and hear, ye sons of Jacob; and hearken unto Israel your father.[35]

On that occasion it was Judah and Joseph who received the important blessings. Beyond all of the other sons, theirs stood out in both length and content. According to the predictions and promises made, they were the ones who would initiate the particular lines of lineage that someday would have the most significant impact upon the House of Israel.

Judah's blessing, for example, was noticeably administrative in nature. He was one whose descendants would become prominent in Israelite leadership, two of the most famous being King David and his son Solomon.

But in the blessing given to Joseph, the emphasis appeared to be more on a numerous posterity whose widespread migrations would take them to many different parts of the earth. The forecast included blessings of "heaven above" and of "the deep that lieth under," as well as those pertaining to a mysterious geographical area designated as "the everlasting hills."

> The blessings of thy father have prevailed above the blessings of my progenitors, unto the utmost bound of the everlasting hills: they shall be on the head of Joseph, and on the crown of the head of him that was separate from his brethren.[36]

This same type of content also appeared in the blessing given later by Moses on the plains of Moab. Although the pronouncement upon Judah at that time was comparatively brief, the one bestowed upon Joseph, including Ephraim and Manasseh, was once more the longest of any of the other tribes' blessings, and also the most varied and detailed.

In Joseph's blessing a numerous posterity was again implied, referring to a people whose future travels would take them to distant parts of the world.

> His glory is like the firstling of his bullock, and his horns are like the horns of unicorns: with them he shall push the people together to the ends of the earth: and they are the ten thousands of Ephraim, and they are the thousands of Manasseh.[37]

In addition, there was a strong emphasis in the blessing on earth and land, on things pertaining to geography, geology and agriculture, including another reference to the "everlasting hills" as well as "ancient mountains." No specific places were mentioned, but a definite implication of remoteness was given, along with scenes far removed and distant. An aura of mystery, in fact, accompanied many of the promises given to this favorite son of Jacob, who during his lifetime was such an important figure and personality.

But one important fact exists in all of these promises, and that is that of Joseph's two sons, it was Ephraim and not Manasseh who inherited the most important blessings. Not only was he granted the Israelite birthright along with his brother, but he was also the one designated as *firstborn* among all of the twelve tribes. And because of an apparent foreordination in premortal life, he was now the forerunner on earth who would initiate a special lineage and line of genealogy and consequently occupy a strategic position within the House of Israel.

Birth of a Nation

When the children of Israel migrated into Egypt from Palestine, according to the Book of Genesis, they were referred to collectively as the House of Jacob. At that point in history they were less than one hundred people in number. Not until the sixteenth chapter of Exodus, after they had developed into a large population and were coming out of Egyptian captivity, are they called the House of Israel for the first time.

Following this initial reference in the Bible, the famous title occurs 145 times, in most instances designating all of the tribes together but in others only a part. In the Book of Ezekiel alone, where the name is most often used, it occurs in a total of 83 places.

Of course, as an earthly organization the twelve tribes also went by the common name of children of Israel, as well as by other titles including *Hebrews, seed of Abraham*, and the *children of promise*. But the more descriptive words, and the ones which the Lord himself used in identifying the people as they journeyed across the Sinai Peninsula, were of a different type, those such as a *peculiar treasure* and a *kingdom of priests*.

> Now therefore, if you will obey my voice indeed, and keep my covenant, then ye shall be a peculiar treasure unto me above all people: for all the earth is mine: and ye shall be unto me a kingdom of priests, and an holy nation.[38]

In journeying toward the promised land, the House of Israel was indeed a priestly nation, a traveling host of people seeking a religious place of refuge and a new homeland. Their destination was not a land foreign to their forefathers, but for those of the new generation, it was a place of intrigue and uncertainty, one inhabited by a race of giants living in strong fortresses and walled cities. It was a place which many before them at Kadesh-Barnea had rejected and refused to enter, and in so doing had suffered unfortunate consequences.

Yet as the second group finally left the plains of Moab and crossed the Jordan River into Canaan, following the new leadership of Joshua, they did so with a different attitude and a renewed determination to possess the land. No longer were they of a disposition to return to Egypt. Now they were determined to go ahead, believing that the Lord was with them and would help them fight their battles. Moreover, they had the comfort of knowing that they were a numerous population and possessed a formidable army of more than a half million men!

As this vast array of people moved across the country that had been promised them, taking one city and place after another, they became the nemesis of every man, woman and child in Palestine. All of those in their path, including Canaanites, Hivites, Perizzites and Jebusites, came under the conquest and domination of the Israelite invaders. Certainly the House of Israel at this time in history was a significant group among the nations, not only with a prestigious heritage and identity, but a large population as well. Their numbers alone made them a significant force to be reckoned with.

Earlier on the plains of Moab when the second census was taken, the number of men twenty years and older had been more than 600,000. Again this was an amount suggesting a total population of two to three million people, approximately the same number that had come out of Egypt. At the same time, however, it was also a figure that would soon undergo a dramatic change. During the time of King David, in fact, some two hundred years or so later, a third census would be taken, showing that the size of the House of Israel had more than doubled.

In other words, following the decline in population which occurred in the wilderness, the Israelites finally arrived at a point where they could experience a more normal growth and increase. At last the nomadic trek across the desert was over, and within the confines of the land of promise, their development as a nation could now progress evenly and uninterrupted. For the first time they would be able to enjoy the benefits of a new homeland. And yet despite the prospects of peace and prosperity, there were definitely troubled days ahead.

After the conquest of Palestine, for example, when Joshua had grown old and passed away, the people would go through a long period of time known as the Judges, followed by the well-known kingships of Saul, David and Solomon. And finally, in fulfillment of predictions made by the prophets, the famous house consisting of twelve tribes would separate into two kingdoms, each one eventually submitting to the conquest of another nation and then dispersing to various parts of the earth.

Joshua

On the day that the children of Israel passed over the Jordan River into Canaan, an unusual event occurred at the place of entry. The river at that time of year was overflowing its banks, and the people were undoubtedly wondering how they would get across. But the Lord gave Joshua a plan ahead of time and told him exactly what to do.

Joshua first instructed the priests carrying the ark of the covenant to step into the river, at which time the oncoming water stopped and raised up in a heap. Then the whole company of Israel crossed the river on dry ground.

It was also at this time that another event took place which again had particular significance in connection with the number of twelve. Following the crossing of the river, the Lord told Joshua to choose one man from each of the twelve tribes in preparation for an important ceremony.

> Take you twelve men out of the people, out of every tribe a man,
>
> And command ye them saying, Take you hence out of the midst of Jordan, out of the place where the priests' feet stood firm, twelve stones, and ye shall carry them over with you, and leave them in the lodging place where ye shall lodge this night.[39]

The idea was to construct a memorial that would remind future generations of what had happened during the historic crossing, in commemoration of an event similar to when the Israelites came out of Egyptian bondage and walked over a passageway through the Red Sea. It would also remind the people that the Lord was still guiding them and was always ready to help them.

In the place called Gilgal, therefore, which was the site of the first camp that evening, Joshua made a mound out of the stones that had been carried there. He also placed twelve stones in the river at the place where the priests carrying the ark had stood. This was part of a continuing symbolism pertaining to the twelve tribes of Israel, in this case representing not just a historic river crossing but the beginning of a new adventure in Palestine. It also gave notice that the man named Joshua had come to the forefront and was now the new leader of the Israelite nation. The man who had been tutored by Moses himself was now the one who would lead the children of Israel into the promised land.

It was also Joshua who was the prestigious member of the tribe of Ephraim, a standing which gave him considerable power and influence. As a direct descendant of Ephraim of old, he was not only the supreme commander of Israel's military forces but the successor to Moses in all religious and ecclesiastical affairs. He was the one that the Lord now spoke to in guiding the affairs of the children of Israel.

> As I was with Moses, so I will be with thee: I will not fail thee, nor forsake thee.

> Be strong and of a good courage; be not afraid, neither be thou dismayed: for the Lord thy God is with thee whithersoever thou goest.[40]

And so it was that across the river, at the site of the twelve stones, the House of Israel commenced another phase in its long illustrious history. From Canaan to Egypt and then back again, the people finally repossessed the land of their inheritance which they had received through Abraham, Isaac and Jacob. Once more they stood on sacred ground where their forefathers had obtained the promises, those which told them that someday they would become a mighty nation and that through them all other nations of the earth would be blessed.

Although Moses was no longer with them, having been taken up by the Lord in the plains of Moab, they now followed the new leadership of the man called Joshua, first taking possession of the land of promise which lay before them and then continuing on toward their destiny!

Invasion and Conquest

The conquest of Canaan by the children of Israel was not easy. In fact, there were certain places which at first were not conquered at all. Not until the time of King David did all of the land actually come under Israelite control.

But Joshua and his forces nevertheless succeeded in subjugating the greater part of Palestine. Territory east of the Jordan River had already been taken and assigned to two and a half of the tribes, and now the same thing occurred in the west. As recorded in the Book of Joshua, thirty-one Canaanite cities, along with their respective kings, all fell before the invading armies.

Following the conquest came the division of territory, preparations for which had taken place earlier on the plains of Moab. Joshua and Eleazar the priest were in charge of the operation, and they were assisted by ten princes representing the remaining nine and a half tribes. "These are they," as stated in the Bible, "whom the Lord commanded to divide the inheritance unto the children of Israel in the land of Canaan."[41]

The division began in Gilgal. Caleb and the tribe of Judah were the first to receive land. Because Caleb had been faithful during the testing period in the wilderness, he was given an area later known as Hebron, the mountain fortress where he overcame the race of giants. After him came the whole company of Judah, who was granted a large expanse of land west of the Dead Sea, including the city of Jerusalem.

Finally, the second and last group to receive an inheritance at Gilgal was the posterity of Joseph: the two tribes of Ephraim and Manasseh. Their territory in central Palestine was close in size to that of Judah's and comprised some of the choicest land, as well as important religious centers such as Bethel and Shiloh. The allotment, however, turned out to be too small for them, in their opinion, and at the very beginning, representatives of both

groups came to Joshua and made a request for additional territory. They were also quick to remind him of their status as tribes
and as a people.

"Why hast thou given me but one lot and one portion to
inherit," they asked, "seeing I am a great people, forasmuch as
the Lord hath blessed me hitherto?" Their present situation and
standing, in other words, should have entitled them to much
more than what they had been given. Not only were they a large
group in number, but they were also well aware of their heritage,
the fact that they had been given the birthright among the tribes
and that Ephraim was designated as firstborn.

But whatever their intent and purpose, the request for extra
land was granted. In addition to the inheritance which they had
already received in Mount Ephraim, Joshua gave them additional territory in a nearby mountainous area. "Thou are a great
people," he told them, "and hast great power: thou shalt not
have one lot only: but the mountain shall be thine."[42]

Joshua's reference to a great people who had great power
included himself, of course, since he was a member of the tribe
of Ephraim. And in granting the additional land, he acknowledged the responsibility which all of them had at that time to
promote a common cause among the Israelite people and
provide an important part of the leadership.

All of this occurred in Gilgal at the place of the twelve stones,
after which the entire congregation of Israel moved to the city of
Shiloh where the division of territory continued. Seven tribes
had yet to receive their inheritance in the land of Canaan, and at
the new location, on historic ground and in front of the tabernacle of the congregation, the final lots were cast. Allotments at
that time were given to Benjamin, Simeon, Zebulun, Issachar,
Asher, Naphtali and Dan.

As far as Joshua was concerned, his personal allotment was
the city of Timnathserah, located in Mount Ephraim. This was
the place which he had requested, and it was assigned to him
after all of the other territory had been divided.

Thus it was that the people of the House of Israel finally

obtained their rightful inheritance. In the same surroundings where Abraham, Isaac and Jacob first received the ancient promises, Joshua and those with him now took possession of the majority of land. The conquest had not been easy, nor was it entirely successful, yet it was enough to give them a permanent location for the next few centuries and an opportunity to develop as a nation in a former place and homeland.

Internal Conflicts

Following the death of Joshua, the Israelites withdrew further and further into separate areas and were soon going their individual ways. Spread over a large expanse of territory and separated in part by the Jordan River, they were no longer unified politically as they had been earlier, but were now a loose confederation of tribes. Any civil government among them, if it could be called such, was a succession of twelve judges at the first, ranging from the time of Othniel to the well-known days of Samson. Only when there was a threat from an outside source were the people apt to band together in a common cause.

The more significant danger was when they had serious conflicts and wars among themselves. On one such occasion, for example, a man named Jephthah of the tribe of Manasseh was hired to lead an army of Gileadites in Transjordan against the neighboring people of Ammon. The latter were making claims to some of the Israelite land. Jephthah was successful in defeating these people, but after the fighting was over, he was met by a large army of men who had crossed over the Jordan River from the tribe of Ephraim.

They were upset because they had not been invited to partic- ipate in the conflict, which Jephthah denied, and they also accused the Gileadites of being fugitives of Ephraim. Then to make matters worse, they threatened to burn Jephthah's house.

In response to all of this, Jephthah and the Gileadites took strong action. They fought the men of Ephraim and defeated them, after which they blocked all passages leading across the river. Their intent was to prevent any of the people from returning to their homes in Mount Ephraim.

This was also the time when the use of a certain password designated as *Shibboleth* was implemented. If anyone tried to cross the river in disguise without it, he was immediately appre- hended and executed. It was an unfortunate situation for the

Ephramites because they could not pronounce the word correctly. Some dialect or manner of speaking had developed within their tribe, and on this occasion it resulted in disaster. This occurred whenever Jephthah and the Gileadites confronted anyone from Ephraim and asked the crucial question.

> Then said they unto him, Say now Shibboleth: and he said Sibboleth: for he could not frame to pronounce it right. Then they took him and slew him at the passages of Jordan.[43]

It definitely was a tragic day in Israelite history, and especially for the tribe of Ephraim, since at the time the conflict was finally over, 42,000 were reportedly killed. Few if any in their entire army survived. Of course, it might be another instance where an error was made in the translation and transcription of the Bible, resulting in the number of deaths being too high. But in any case, such a thing within the family of Israel should never have happened, and for it to occur within a tribe so preeminent as Ephraim, it was particularly sad and humiliating.

The same was also true sometime later when another event took place which was likewise a tragedy, one that again happened among the tribes themselves. It first occurred in the territory of Benjamin and then spread quickly to the other tribes.

A few of the Benjaminites who were known as the *sons of Belial* committed a serious crime, and when the rest of Israel heard about it, they demanded that those who were guilty be brought forward and punished. But the leaders of Benjamin refused, and as a result, a conflict soon developed between the two groups.

From the city of Dan in the north to Beersheba in the south, an army of 400,000 Israelites, according to the Bible, gathered together to go against the dissenting tribe. Benjamin had a force of only 26,700, and yet as things turned out, it was no easy task to overcome them.

But after three attempts, in which there were heavy casualties on both sides, the combined tribes finally emerged victorious, the result being almost the complete annihilation of the tribe of Benjamin. Only six hundred men remained, and these fled to a place in the wilderness called the rock of Rimmon.

Once more it was a day of infamy for the House of Israel, a day in which a terrible breach was made within the twelve tribes. And like the earlier event, it left another scar that could not easily be erased.

> And the people came to the house of God, and abode there till even before God, and lifted up their voices, and wept sore; and said, O Lord God of Israel, why is this come to pass in Israel, that there should be today one tribe lacking in Israel?[44]

Despite Benjamin's downfall, however, the other tribes determined to mend the breach by providing a way for the surviving soldiers to marry and continue having families, thus preserving the tribe in question and keeping the House of Israel intact. It took some devious and unusual maneuvering, but the tribal leaders eventually managed to find the right number of wives for the fugitives who had temporarily exiled themselves at the rock of Rimmon.

What happened proved to be a strange interlude in Israelite history, one involving the abduction of 400 unmarried women from a rebellious Israelite city and another the kidnapping of 200 girls who were attending a religious feast, all for the purpose of obtaining the necessary wives. Indeed, in very few places in the Bible is there a more bizarre situation, although it did provide the solution to a serious problem. Yet even though the tribes of Israel were kept intact, there was still no assurance that other internal conflicts would not occur in the future, striking at the very foundation of the House of Israel.

Certainly the possibility of other dangerous occurrences was always present. The two unfortunate events so far, one pertaining to Ephraim and the other to Benjamin, were continuing reminders that the Israelites lacked unity and that unless some kind of change was made, the twelve tribes could one day disappear as an institution, each tribe permanently going its own way. The need for a stronger form of government was definitely implied. In fact, the time was coming not too far in the future when a petition would be made by all of the tribal elders requesting the discontinuation of the rule of the judges and the inauguration of Israel's first king.

Israelite Monarchy

In addition to the conflicts which occurred among the twelve tribes, there were at least two other events contributing to the end of the judges. During a battle with the Philistines, for example, the Israelites temporarily lost the ark of the covenant, something which had never happened before and an occurrence which caused great anxiety. Then sometime later, in the days of Samuel, the prophet's two sons began abusing their priestly office, and the people finally made up their minds that now was the time to have a king, like those in other nations surrounding them.

While coming out of Egypt, the Israelite government had been designated by the Lord as a spiritual type of monarchy, "a kingdom of priests, and an holy nation." But now the people wanted that kind of government politically as well. They desired a strong ruler who would be their judge and also go before them to fight their battles.

As a result, a man named Saul was anointed by Samuel to become the first Israelite king. He was an outstanding individual from the tribe of Benjamin and came from a very prominent family. "And there was not among the children of Israel a goodlier person than he," states the Bible, and "from his shoulders and upward he was higher than any of the people."[45]

But despite Saul's ability and accomplishments, he changed during his kingship and ended his reign with a troubled mind and spirit, characterized by extreme jealousy and an unstable disposition. Indeed, he eventually spent much of his time trying to slay the man who was anointed to succeed him as king. This was David of the tribe of Judah, the one who killed Goliath and a man idolized by the Israelite people.

It was David, in fact, who was not only Israel's second king and ruler but was also a brilliant military strategist who finally completed the conquest of Canaan. Under his leadership, the

Israelite armies expanded the borders of the kingdom until they encompassed the entire area given to Abraham, Isaac and Jacob. Certainly it was an impressive expanse of territory, extending from beyond the Jordan River to most of the country bordering the eastern end of the Mediterranean Sea, as well as from the Euphrates River in the north to the river of Egypt in the south.

And yet politically, during the time of David and even before his reign, there were signs that the House of Israel already had begun to separate into two groups, culturally as well as geographically. At one point in the Bible, for example, while David was still a military commander, it states that Israelites in two strategic areas, Israel in the north and Judah in the south, were well pleased with him, not only because of his victories on the battlefield but because he was genuinely concerned about the people and acted in their behalf.

> But all Israel and Judah loved David, because he went out and came in before them.[46]

The powerful tribe of Judah and part of the tribe of Benjamin in southern Palestine, and eventually the people of Levi, were mainly those who were designated as Judah. Most of the other tribes, including Ephraim and Manasseh, generally retained the name of Israel. No specific reason is given as to why such a division took place, but a well-known biblical prophecy stated that someday in the future Ephraim would no longer envy Judah, and Judah not vex Ephraim. Along with economic and geographic reasons, in other words, there also appears to have been significant cultural differences between the two groups.

In any case, Israel and Judah existed separately to a large extent, and when Saul's reign came to an end, after a tragic series of events, David became the new king of Judah, and Ishbosheth, a son of Saul, was made king of Israel. For several years there was war between the house of David and the house of Saul, and then after a short time, when David had established himself as the more successful ruler, he eventually obtained control of the entire kingdom "over Israel and over Judah, from Dan even to Beersheba."[47]

It was in those days, during the forty years of David's kingship, that the twelve tribes of Israel finally reached their greatest height. Politically and economically, as well as geographically, they secured a strong and significant position among the surrounding nations of the Middle East.

They likewise showed a remarkable increase in population growth. According to one report in a third census that was taken during David's administration, Judah was credited with a fighting force of 500,000 men, while Israel claimed a total of 800,000. In another report, the amount was even greater, Judah showing 470,000 and Israel 1,100,000. Based on the information contained in these two sources, a calculated population of men, women and children could have been as much as five million people or more, given the possibility that in the recording of numbers, translation and transcription problems again might have existed.[48]

Certainly the House of Israel was going through significant changes, including a rapid growth in numbers. Also for the first time, the twelve tribes were firmly situated on Israelite soil. Many of the prophecies made concerning the children of Israel were now being fulfilled, and following David's death, the prospects for the future seemed very favorable, continuing to the time of his son Solomon, who became Israel's third king.

In some ways, in fact, it was during Solomon's reign that Israel achieved its most impressive image and stature.

> Judah and Israel were many, as the sand which is by the sea in multitude, eating and drinking, and making merry.

It was a time when

> Solomon reigned over all kingdoms from the river unto the land of the Philistines, and unto the border of Egypt.

> And Judah and Israel dwelt safely, every man under his vine and under his fig tree, from Dan even to Beersheba, all the days of Solomon.[49]

Solomon inherited many things from his father, of course, as far as the kingdom was concerned, but he also added much on his own, his most outstanding achievement being the construction of the magnificent temple in Jerusalem. He was also known for his great wisdom, a gift and talent given to him by the Lord. Indeed, people came from many different lands and countries to listen to his counsel, including those of very high standing.

> And all the kings of the earth sought the presence of Solomon, to hear his wisdom that God had put in his heart.

Probably the most famous and most publicized of these visits was that of the Queen of Sheba, and from her evaluation of Solomon and his kingdom come additional views and information.

> It was a true report, which I heard in mine own land of thine acts and of thy wisdom: howbeit I believed not their words until I came and mine eyes had seen it: and behold the one half of the greatness of thy wisdom was not told me: for thou exceedest the fame that I heard.

> Happy are thy men, and happy are these thy servants which stand continually before thee and hear thy wisdom.[50]

But despite all of his knowledge and worthwhile accomplishments, Solomon followed in the way of his two predecessors and eventually strayed from the commandments of the Lord. He also abused the idea that they were not only leaders of their people but in actuality were the spiritual guardians of the House of Israel.

In Solomon's case, it was a love for strange women and his thousand wives and concubines that proved to be his downfall. He turned to practices of idolatry, building forbidden places of worship and allowing his wives to burn incense and make sacrifices to their gods. Truly it was an unexpected outcome for one who had been such a unique and outstanding ruler. As a consequence, his actions would one day be followed by a very tragic event that had been threatening for years, a devastating schism among the Israelite people and a permanent division within Israel's twelve tribes.

Division of an Empire

At the time that Solomon dedicated the new temple in Jerusalem, he had called in the twelve princes, one from each of the tribes, to help celebrate the occasion. It was one of the last times these men would be gathered together as a group, since already on the horizon there were signs that a united Israel was coming to an end.

Ever since the time of Moses the princes had been an integral part of the House of Israel, symbolizing the character and unity of the twelve tribes and performing various governmental and ecclesiastical functions. And although they were less of a factor during the period of the judges, their presence was again made known in the time of David and Solomon.

It is uncertain, however, as to how much power and influence these men actually had in connection with all of the tribes collectively. Each prince undoubtedly possessed considerable authority within his own tribe, but especially during the period of monarchy their role as advisors within the larger group, as well as that of voting members, was probably much more limited.

This appeared to be true when Solomon died and his son Rehoboam became king. Instead of consulting with tribal leaders on an important question, for example, he turned to those of his own court and others immediately surrounding him.

The question was how to proceed in governing the people, particularly the ten tribes who collectively were known as Israel. The tribes had already pledged their allegiance and support to the new king, but only on condition that he would improve their situation as far as taxation and other matters were concerned.

> Thy father made our yoke grievous, Now therefore make thou the grievous service of thy father, and his heavy yoke which he put upon us, lighter and we will serve thee.[51]

Rehoboam asked for three days to think it over and in the

meantime consulted first with the older men who had been advisors to his father, and after that with younger men his own age. And although the first group counseled him to grant Israel's request, he chose to accept the advice of the second which said he should be more aggressive and adopt a more authoritative policy.

As a result, the new ruler treated Israel very roughly when he saw them again and gave them his unfortunate decision. "My father made your yoke heavy," he said, "and I will add to your yoke: my father also chastised you with whips, but I will chastise you with scorpions."[52]

It is difficult to imagine Rehoboam acting in such a manner, and the result, of course, was instantaneous rebellion. The ten tribes of Israel, who were led by a man named Jeroboam, immediately departed from the king and let it be known that they would no longer have anything to do with the house of David.

"What portion have we in David?" they asked, referring to the king they had once served and admired. "Neither have we inheritance in the son of Jesse."

"To your tents, O Israel!" they cried. "Now see to thine own house, David!"[53]

Such an event certainly was not unprecedented. These same words, in fact, had been spoken on an earlier occasion when King David was returning to the city of Jerusalem, having temporarily vacated the capital when his son Absalom tried to take over the kingdom. The royal party had just crossed the Jordan River to Gilgal when an angry group of men from the ten tribes appeared and confronted the tribe of Judah and others who were serving as escorts.

"We have ten parts in the king," they said, "and we have also more right in David than ye: why then did ye despise us, that our advice should not be first had in bringing back our king?"

But the men of Judah refuted them, saying they had done no wrong and that Israel had no cause for being upset.

It was a tense moment, one taken advantage of by a certain man named Sheba from the tribe of Benjamin who suddenly blew a trumpet and gave a signal to the others. "We have no part in David," he shouted. "Neither have we inheritance in the son of Jesse. Every man to his tents, O Israel!"[54] And at that time, everyone in the group left King David and went his own way.

Fortunately in those days, this initial rebellion was only temporary, yet it was the forerunner of the one to come, that which occurred at the time that Rehoboam became king. Actually it was only one of several incidents occurring down through the years showing that Israel and Judah were on different paths and that a permanent rift sometime in the future was inevitable.

In addition, there was also the idea that the Lord himself was operating behind the scenes. Prior to the rebellion, for example, the prophet Ahijah had taken Jeroboam to the side one day and given him an important message. Jeroboam, who was a member of the tribe of Ephraim, was to be the new king of the Kingdom of Israel, the prophet said, with Solomon's son Rehoboam as king of the Kingdom of Judah.

To illustrate and dramatize this coming event, Ahijah took a new coat that Jeroboam was wearing and ripped it into twelve pieces, ten of which he handed back to its owner.

> Take thee ten pieces, for thus saith the Lord, the God of Israel, Behold, I will rend the kingdom out of the hand of Solomon and will give ten tribes to thee.

> And unto his son will I give one tribe, that David my servant may have a light alway before me in Jerusalem, the city which I have chosen to put my name there.[55]

Sometime later, after Solomon died and the ten tribes had revolted, still another event took place which again involved divine intervention. On that second occasion, the new king Rehoboam assembled a large army from the tribes of Judah and Benjamin and prepared to go to war against the other tribes, thinking he could force them to remain in the kingdom and keep the House of Israel intact. But a prophet stopped him at the last moment and gave him the Lord's instructions.

"Thus saith the Lord," the prophet told him, "ye shall not go up, nor fight against your brethren the children of Israel: return every man to his house: for this thing is from me."

In other words, "the cause was from the Lord," that "he might perform his saying" which he had earlier given to Ahijah.[56] For whatever reason, he was allowing the revolution of the tribes to continue, revealing the way that things were meant to be. And although Rehoboam would have preferred it otherwise, it was obviously too late for a change, and Solomon's magnificent kingdom and empire were divided forever.

The House of Israel, which had managed to stay together since the time that Jacob and his family came out of the land of Mesopotamia, now unfortunately became two kingdoms instead of one, and as a result, the phenomenon referred to in the Bible as the scattering of Israel finally came into existence.

Two Separate Kingdoms

Although it is customary to refer to the Kingdom of Israel as having ten tribes, originally there were more like eleven and a half. These included Reuben, Simeon, Dan, Naphtali, Gad, Asher, Issachar, Zebulun, Ephraim and Manasseh, and also the tribe of Levi and part of Benjamin. The kingdom was located mainly in northern and central Palestine, as well as Transjordan, with capitals first at Shechem and Tirzah, and later in Samaria.

This left the southern kingdom with the tribe of Judah and the remaining part of Benjamin, the capital city being Jerusalem.

But as time went by, the composition of the tribes changed and became more solidified. In the north, for example, when Jeroboam introduced certain religious innovations and idolatrous practices, the tribe of Levi transferred to the kingdom in the south. Actually the people were expelled by an order from the king who replaced them with a priesthood of his own.

Moreover, there were those among the people of Dan who also chose to join with Judah, along with many from the other groups whose religious feelings inclined them more toward the southern kingdom than the north.

In any case, the division of tribes, which occurred soon after Solomon's death in approximately 930 B.C., eventually became complete, and during the next four centuries, Judah was ruled by a total of twenty kings and Israel by nineteen, among them being such well-known figures as Ahab, Jehu, Jehoshaphat, and Hezekiah. These were also the days of the famous prophets Elijah, Isaiah and Jeremiah.

Throughout their history as kingdoms, the two groups existed side by side, each going its own way and occasionally coming into conflict with one another. Despite their kinship and common heritage, they continued to have serious problems and even open warfare. A dispute between them was possible at any time, and it was not uncommon on some of these occasions for the tribe of Ephraim to be at the center of difficulty.

Such an incident occurred at a time when a man named Amaziah was king of Judah. On one occasion, while preparing to go to battle against the neighboring Edomites, he assembled an army of 300,000 men from the tribes of Judah and Benjamin and then hired an additional 100,000 from the tribe of Ephraim. At the last minute, however, on the advice of a prophet, he decided not to use Ephraim's forces after all, and upon their release they became very upset.

> Then Amaziah separated them, to wit, the army that was come to him out of Ephraim, to go home again: wherefore their anger was greatly kindled against Judah, and they returned home in great anger.[57]

As a result, the returning Ephraimites ravaged some of the cities of Judah between Bethhoron and Samaria, killing 3,000 people and taking "much spoil."

And then, as if this were not enough, Amaziah later invited the king of Israel himself to meet with him on the field of battle at a place called Bethshemesh. Having recently been successful in dealing with the Edomites, he was apparently confident he could be victorious again. But things did not turn out that way, and Amaziah and his forces suffered a humiliating defeat at the hands of their Israelite kinsmen.

Following his victory the king of Israel, whose name was Johoash, then went to Jerusalem and broke down the city wall, "from the gate of Ephraim unto the corner gate, four hundred cubits. And he took all the gold and silver, and all the vessels that were found in the house of the Lord, and in the treasures of the king's house, the hostages, and returned to Samaria."[58]

Certainly it was another reminder of the unfortunate circumstances which beset the two kingdoms of Israel and Judah. Incidents of one kind or another occurred all through their history, always accentuating the differences between them. And yet the real danger to both, as far as their future destinies were concerned, was not the presence of internal difficulties but rather a danger coming from a different direction. Already on the horizon there were signs of an approaching storm, this time a threat posed by surrounding nations.

Certain cultures and societies, especially in the north, were developing into strong empires and would eventually come down onto the tribes of Israel like a cloud, conquering both kingdoms and uprooting much of their population. In a very methodical manner, they would subjugate the Palestinian and Transjordanian cities and bring to an end their coveted independence and autonomy.

Undoubtedly it would be the worst time in all of Israelite history. From the days of Egyptian bondage to the long exodus in the wilderness, and then down through the difficult centuries in the promised land, there was nothing that would equal the coming invasions of northern armies. The Israelite territory that had once been a land flowing with milk and honey would soon become a virtual battleground, after which the House of Israel would be completely dismembered and scattered to many different parts of the earth!

Assyrian Conquests

The first Israelite kingdom to be invaded and conquered by a foreign power was the Kingdom of Israel. Armies coming out of the Assyrian Empire in the north took first one part of the kingdom and then another and added both to a growing list of subservient nations. Assyria had become the dominant force in the Middle East and showed no mercy to anyone who would not pay homage and tribute.

These two conquests, which occurred during the latter part of the 8th century B.C., were particularly significant in connection with the House of Israel because they produced a society known as the *ten lost tribes*. This was a group that eventually separated themselves from those taken into Assyrian captivity and traveled to an unidentified location somewhere in the north country. Here they completely disappeared, and since that time anything pertaining to their existence has remained a mystery. Indeed, in very few places in all of Israelite history is there a situation as unique and unusual as that pertaining to this particular group of people.

In regard to the conquests themselves, however, the first one to occur was the subjugation of Transjordan and northern Palestine by the Assyrian king Tiglath-Pileser III. This took place in about 733 B.C., after which the territory was annexed to the Assyrian Empire and part of its population deported to foreign cities in the north. At that time a man named Pekah was king of the Kingdom of Israel.

Pekah and his forces had earlier gone to war against neighboring Judah, killing 120,000 people in one day, according to the Bible, and temporarily taking 200,000 men, women, and children captive. Ironically, it was a preview of what was to happen to the Kingdom of Israel itself at the hands of the Assyrians.

In the days of Pekah, king of Israel, came Tiglath-Pileser, king of Assyria, and took Ijon, and Abelbethmaachah, and Janoah, and Kedesh, and Hazor, and Gilead, and Galilee, all the land of Naphtali, and carried them captive to Assyria.

And he carried them away, even the Reubenites, and the Gadites, and half the tribe of Manasseh, and brought them unto Halah, and Habor, and Hara, and to the river Gozan, unto this day.[59]

Besides the tribes of Reuben, Gad, and part of Manasseh, the conquered regions also contained people from the tribes of Asher, Zebulun, Naphtali, Issachar and Dan. Certainly it resulted in a widespread removal of people, although again there were many among the different populations who still remained.

It was Assyrian policy during this time period not to deport the entire population of an area but only about one-half. Then by bringing in colonists from other parts of the empire to take their place, the new rulers weakened the existing social structure and were able to maintain a stronger control.[60]

Also the people that were actually taken appear to have been mostly from the upper classes, including political and ecclesiastical leaders, artisans, and those from the aristocracy. Anyone who was from the lower classes, therefore, was more apt to be left behind.

Such a policy constituted an important factor in the conquest of the Kingdom of Israel and the ten tribes, which means that many were deported, but many others were left in their own lands to intermingle with incoming colonists, eventually developing into hybrid groups.

The same was also true at the time of the second Assyrian conquest. In approximately 724 B.C., the armies of the north again entered Palestine, bypassing the Kingdom of Judah but devastating a more rebellious Kingdom of Israel. The Assyrian king on this occasion was Shalmaneser V, and the unfortunate ruler in Israel was a man named Hoshea.

> Then the king of Assyria came up throughout all the land and went up to Samaria and besieged it three years. In the ninth year of Hoshea, the king of Assyria took Samaria, and carried Israel away into Assyria, and placed them in Halah and in Habor by the river Gozan, and in the cities of the Medes.[61]

The Israelites on this occasion held out much longer than might have been expected, but as the capital city finally fell to the invaders in 721 B.C., it sounded a death knell, and the history of the Kingdom of Israel came to a close.

It was also during this same time period that Assyria changed kings, and Sargon II became the new ruler. He actually appears to have been the one who concluded the conquest of Samaria. After traveling to Egypt for additional campaigns, he returned some two years later, according to one account, stopping in Israel on the way home and taking more than 27,000 of the people captive, all of whom were deported in the usual manner to different parts of the Assyrian Empire.

In an inscription which commemorated this event, Sargon left the following account:

> The man of Samaria and a king who was hostile to me had joined together to refuse homage and tribute to me, and came out to fight with me. By the help of the great gods, my lords, I overthrew them: I captured from them 27,280 persons with their chariots, their gods in whom they trusted, and took as my royal share of the booty 200 chariots. I gave orders that the rest should be settled in the midst of Assyria.[62]

Again the prisoners taken appear to have been mostly from the upper classes, the people's intelligentsia, so to speak, that the Assyrians were evidently thinking about as far as potential trouble and insurrection were concerned. And like the others during the invasion before them, the captives were removed and new colonists brought in to take their place.

> So was Israel carried away out of their own land to Assyria unto this day. And the king of Assyria brought men from Babylon, and from Cuthah, and from Ava, and from Hamath, and from Sepharvaim, and placed them in the cities of Samaria instead of the children of Israel: and they possessed Samaria and dwelt in the cities thereof.[63]

It is interesting that the prophet Jeremiah, in connection with the Assyrian invasions, referred to the conquered population as Ephraim rather than Israel. The reason was because Ephraim in many ways was the kingdom's most prominent tribe, and consequently its name was often used to designate the entire group.

Following the invasions, for example, Jeremiah warned the Kingdom of Judah to the south that if it continued its waywardness, it would suffer a fate similar to Israel. "And I will cast you out of my sight," he said, speaking for the Lord, "as I have cast out all your brethren, even the whole seed of Ephraim."[64] The prophets Isaiah and Hosea also referred to Israel in this manner.

Thus the so-called seed of Ephraim, or Kingdom of Israel, finally ceased to exist as a united people and nation. A population which had been together for more than 200 years was now separated into two groups, one that remained in the original homeland of Palestine and Transjordan and the other dispersed to various parts of the Assyrian Empire, mainly between the upper reaches of the Tigris and Euphrates Rivers not far from the city of Nineveh. Additional captivity sites, mentioned only as the cities of the Medes, were located farther to the east.

In a distant locality, therefore, a large part of the ten tribes spent many years in captivity, a period of time generally undetected in Israelite history. Unlike the exiles from the Kingdom of Judah who later would be taken captive into Babylonia, an account of their stay in Assyria is relatively unknown. And for possibly more than a century, they were prisoners in a foreign land, fulfilling all of the predictions which had been made earlier by the prophets.

But again there were signs of change, and the reign of Assyria itself eventually came to an end. A people known as the Chaldeans rose to power in Mesopotamia, initiating a new period in Middle Eastern history and creating a new political situation, one that might partially explain why some of the Israelite captives were suddenly able to turn their backs on the ruling powers and walk away.

According to the biblical record known as the Apocrypha, which is the only documentation for this particular event, at least some of those who had been taken captive banded together and migrated to a new area. These were the ones later to be called the ten lost tribes. Crossing the Euphrates River, they soon turned toward the north and after traveling for eighteen months in an unknown land called Arzareth, arrived at an undetermined location where they completely disappeared. Since then they have become a strange and unusual enigma in biblical history and one of many unsolved mysteries.

Once again, however, not all of the original ten tribes disappeared. Some might have remained in captivity in Mesopotamia or dropped out during the subsequent northern journey, while many others were still back in Palestine mixing with incoming colonists. In any case, the House of Israel continued to be divided and scattered, with an increasing number of its people dispersing to foreign places and finding themselves in new and different circumstances. Indeed, the predicted scattering of Israel was now in full sway and would yet be supplemented by another catastrophic event not too far in the future: the dissolution of the Kingdom of Judah and the complete disappearance of Israelite autonomy in the promised land.

An Interval of Peace

During the two Assyrian conquests in the Kingdom of Israel, a man named Ahaz was king of Judah. At one time, because of the existing political situation, he decided to send to Tiglath-Pileser III in Assyria for help. In those days he was being besieged by Syria, Edom, and the Philistines, as well as by nearby Israel.

The Assyrians responded by attacking the Syrian capital of Damascus, slaying the king and taking the city's inhabitants captive. It was also during this time period that the subjugation of northern Palestine and Transjordan took place.

In return for military assistance, Ahaz paid an expensive tribute to Assyria, taking gold and silver from the house of the Lord and from the treasures of the king's house. Moreover, he broke the temple vessels into pieces and also relocated the large molten sea which Solomon had placed upon the backs of twelve brazen oxen, all for the purpose of giving presents and tribute to the King of Assyria.

By doing this, Judah protected itself from Assyrian conquests, a condition which generally continued during the reign of five successive rulers. The one exception was during the time of Hezekiah when many of the Israelite cities were captured and the capital city of Jerusalem threatened. But this particular crisis passed, and the invading armies eventually returned home.

For a considerable length of time during the reigns of Ahaz, Hezekiah, Manasseh and Amon, the Kingdom of Judah was relatively free from any serious Assyrian oppression. This was also true of the following reign of Josiah, during whose kingship Judah experienced more than thirty years of peace. In this later period, in fact, it seemed for a time that the southern kingdom might actually survive, despite the troubled situation in the Middle East and a continuing threat from Assyria.

One of the main reasons for this, of course, was Josiah himself. The king's reign was very successful, and although he started at a young age, he was an effective administrator from the beginning, eventually becoming one of Judah's most important rulers. Certainly in many ways he was much like Hezekiah who had ruled so well more than a half century before him.

Both kings were exceptionally good men and had many things in common, one of them being a special passover feast which they held in Jerusalem. These were unusual events for the time, and in Josiah's case, his feast turned out to be even more impressive than that of his predecessor.

> And there was no passover like to that kept in Israel from the days of Samuel the prophet; neither did all the kings of Israel keep such a passover as Josiah kept, and the priests, and the Levites, and all Judah and Israel that were present, and the inhabitants of Jerusalem.[65]

Like Hezekiah had done earlier, the king sent people throughout the kingdom, purging different places of all forms of foreign worship and idolatry. He then proceeded to cleanse and repair the temple, or house of the Lord, since the actions of former rulers made it necessary to make renovations and changes.

It was also apparent at this time that there were still significant remnants of population left over from previous Assyrian invasions. People from the original ten tribes were obviously present throughout the length and breadth of Palestine, "in the cities of Manasseh and Ephraim, and Simeon, even unto Naphtali."

This was evident on one occasion during preparations for repairing the temple when it was stated that funds were gathered from "Manasseh and Ephraim, and of all the remnant of Israel, and of all Judah and Benjamin."[66]

Also during Hezekiah's reign, there had been the same type of references to those who had survived Assyrian captivity. In preparing for his own passover feast, the king sent letters of invitation throughout all Israel and Judah saying, "Ye children of

Israel, turn again unto the Lord God of Abraham, Isaac, and Israel, and he will return to the remnant of you that are escaped out of the hand of the kings of Assyria. For if ye turn again unto the Lord, your brethren and your children shall find compassion before them that led them captive, so that they shall come again into this land."

Messengers took Hezekiah's invitation to many different parts of the country, to Simeon in the south and northward through the territories of Ephraim and Manasseh, even as far as Issachar, Asher and Zebulun. And although some of the people "laughed them to scorn and mocked them," there were others who "humbled themselves and came to Jerusalem."[67]

All of this proved to be a welcome interlude of peace, and especially as a result of Josiah's successful reign, it appeared that all was well in the Kingdom of Judah and that things were going in the right direction. There were apparently no serious domestic problems and generally no outside threat of invasion. And possibly things would have continued that way had it not been for the king's untimely death. In what seemed like an unnecessary confrontation with Egypt, which had recently become a dominant force in the Palestinian area, Josiah was fatally wounded during a battle in the Valley of Megiddo.

Certainly few things could have happened in those days that were more destructive to the Kingdom of Judah. Almost immediately the political situation changed. The people quickly anointed Jehoahaz, one of Josiah's sons, and made him king, yet within three months the unfortunate youth was in military custody and on his way to Egypt. Necho, the Egyptian pharaoh who earlier had fought with Josiah at Megiddo, now interjected himself into Israelite affairs and selected a new king of his own, at the same time imposing a tribute.

In the place of Jehoahaz he installed Eliakim, another of Josiah's sons, and changed his name to Jehoiakim. He then took Jehoahaz into Egypt where the deposed king remained until his death.

During this time period, Necho appeared to be the main

political authority in the Palestinian area before eventually relinquishing it to a new power in the north, namely the people known as the Chaldeans of Babylonia.

In connection with these events, Jehoiakim and the Kingdom of Judah first submitted to the power of the Egyptian pharaoh and then later to the Chaldeans. In addition, they were besieged by various bands of Syrians, Moabites and Ammonites. And yet the real threat, as things turned out, was not Egypt or any of the nearby nations, but the Chaldean king whose name was Nebuchadnezzar. He was the one who would soon prove to be Judah's last assailant and nemesis, the one who would finally disrupt the kingdom and bring it to a close, taking many of its people into captivity and dealing still another devastating blow to the beleaguered House of Israel.

The Last Days of Judah

According to the Second Book of Kings in the Bible, Jehoiakim ruled Judah for eleven years and upon his death was buried in Jerusalem. This is also substantiated in the writings of the prophet Jeremiah. Yet in Second Chronicles, the record states that the Chaldeans came down and put Jehoiakim in chains, presumably taking him to Babylon.

But whatever actually happened, Jehoiakim's rule was a stormy one and eventually came to an end after he made an agreement with the Chaldeans and then decided to rebel against Nebuchadnezzar, an action very likely influenced by Egyptian politics. This was also the time period when the first group of prisoners, including Daniel, was taken into captivity and the king's son Jehoiachin was later appointed to be the next king of Judah.

The new kingship, however, turned out to be another brief reign, and after only three months Nebuchadnezzar besieged the city of Jerusalem. He took Jehoiachin captive to Babylon, along with his "mother, and the king's wives, and his officers, and the mighty of the land." Also included were princes, craftsmen and smiths, or anyone who might prove to be a problem politically if left behind. The prophet Ezekiel was also part of this group. "None remained," states the Bible, "save the poorest sort of the people of the land."[68]

In addition, the Chaldeans confiscated the treasures from the house of the Lord, as well as those from the king's palace. They cut in pieces all of the golden vessels which Solomon had made for the temple and took everything with them as they returned to Babylon.

In doing this, Nebuchadnezzar initiated the second phase of the Babylonian Captivity, which also marked the beginning of the end for the Kingdom of Judah. Again all that had been predicted by the prophets now took place. And as the Chaldean king left the city, he appointed Mattaniah, another son of Josiah, to be Judah's twentieth and final king and changed his name to Zedekiah.

This was the situation at the beginning of the 6th Century B.C., and as the new ruler took over, he still had the opportunity to establish an effective policy and save Judah as a kingdom and nation. The prophet Jeremiah especially was advising the king and all of his people to submit to the Chaldeans, which was what Zedekiah initially agreed to do, yet eventually he returned to the ways of Jehoiakim before him, disregarding the counsel of the prophets and relying heavily on the possibility that he could get help and assistance from the pharaoh of Egypt.

At the first of his reign he took an oath and made an agreement with Nebuchadnezzar to serve him but then later changed his mind and rebelled. As a result, the Chaldean armies again came down and attacked Jerusalem, this time making sure that the Kingdom of Judah did not survive.

There was always the possibility that the Egyptian pharaoh could have helped Zedekiah had he wanted to. In the Bible, for example, one account tells of an army from Egypt making an appearance in the vicinity of Jerusalem while the city was being attacked, causing the Chaldeans to temporarily withdraw. But Jeremiah made it clear that the danger was still there, and he gave a vivid reminder of the holocaust that was about to take place.

> For though ye had smitten the whole army of the Chaldeans that fight against you," he said, "and there remained but wounded men among them, yet should they rise up every man in his tent and burn this city with fire.[69]

And that is exactly what happened! Nebuchadnezzar soon returned, and after besieging Jerusalem for eighteen months, his forces entered the city which at the time was suffering not only from military attack but also from severe famine. The Israelite capital was then conquered and devastated, all of its buildings eventually being burned with fire. Everything occurred according to the prophecies of Jeremiah, and in approximately 586 B.C. the once proud Kingdom of Judah finally came to an end.

In the meantime, Zedekiah and his men of war fled from the city by night through a secret gate but were soon overtaken by the Chaldeans on the plains of Jericho. It was at this point that the army was scattered from the king, after which he was taken to a place north of Jerusalem called Riplah where Nebuchadnezzar was waiting for him. Here the final judgments took place, and members of the royal court and family were executed.

The Chaldean king slew Zedekiah's sons before him, as well as his nobles and princes, and then put out the king's eyes and carried him to Babylon. It was a very unfortunate ending, but nevertheless one that had been predicted by the prophet.

Finally, one month after the conquest, the Chaldeans proceeded to destroy the city of Jerusalem. The forces of Nebuzaradan, a captain of the guard appointed by Nebuchadnezzar, burned the temple of Solomon, the king's palace, and all of the houses and buildings. They then tore down the city walls.

> And the pillars of brass that were in the house of the Lord, and the bases, and the brasen sea that was in the house of the Lord, did the Chaldees break in pieces, and carried the brass of them to Babylon.[70]

One of the positive things which took place, however, at the time that Jerusalem was first taken, was Jeremiah's release from prison. The captain of the guard had received specific instructions from Nebuchadnezzar to treat the prophet kindly and provide for his welfare. "Take him, and look well to him," he said, "and do him no harm; but do unto him even as he shall say unto thee."[71]

Jeremiah had earlier been in a dungeon, living under extremely poor conditions, before being put in an area called the court of the prison. It was here that Nebuzaradan found him, and the words which the Chaldean spoke to him on that occasion are some of the most impressive recorded in the Bible.

> And now, behold, I loose thee this day from the chains which were upon thine hand. If it seem good unto thee to come with me into Babylon, come; and I will look well unto thee: but if it seem ill unto thee to come with me into Babylon, forbear: behold, all the land is before thee: whither it seemeth good and convenient for thee to go, thither go.[72]

It was also at this time that Nebuzaradan completed the evacuation of Judah and the city of Jerusalem. Again it was mainly the upper classes of people, according to the Bible, that were taken into captivity while those who were poor were left behind. Jeremiah, of course, chose to stay with the second group.

In addition, there were certain others, among them the king's daughters, men referred to as captains of the forces, and "all the remnant of Judah that were returned from all nations whither they had been driven, to dwell in the land of Judah."[73]

Certainly it was a tragic conclusion to an event that had been building for centuries. The demise of the Kingdom of Judah, along with the destruction of its historic capital, established yet another landmark in the turbulent stream of Israelite history. Since the time of Moses and the exodus from Egypt, the covenant people of the Lord had been warned many times of what would happen if they persisted in their wayward paths, and now all that had been predicted had come true.

Judah and Israel both stood as disinherited kingdoms, and as separate groups of people in the future they would continue to be divided again and again, intermarrying and mixing with the different nations of the earth and becoming a leaven, as it were, among all mankind. Indeed, they had become a severed and scattered population. Yet in the process, they were never forgotten, always remembered by the Lord as his chosen people and retaining the special heritage and promises which they held from the beginning.

I will not utterly destroy the house of Jacob, For lo, I will command, and I will sift the house of Israel among all nations, like as corn is sifted in a sieve, yet shall not the least grain fall upon the earth.[74]

Such was the Lord's declaration and promise to the two Israelite kingdoms, each of which now went its separate way and initiated a very different course in history. Each became the genesis of a new and sometimes undetermined lineage of posterity. Through the centuries of time, for example, the account of the tribe of Judah and those associated with it was usually fairly well-defined, but that of Israel remained much more obscure and unknown. The people in the latter kingdom, in fact, especially when they intermingled with other groups, eventually lost their Israelite identity, while those among the ten tribes that traveled into the north country disappeared completely.

It is impossible to know in how many different directions the people went. The number of dispersions and migrations undoubtedly were many. One such reference is found in a record called The Book of Mormon, which focuses heavily upon the affairs of the House of Israel. It states that many of those leaving the vicinity of the original homeland traveled to distant lands and continents, regarded also as the isles of the sea.

And behold, there are many who are already lost from the knowledge of those who are at Jerusalem. Yea, the more part of all the tribes have been led away; and they are scattered to and fro upon the isles of the sea; and whither they are none of us knoweth, save that we know that they have been led away.

For behold, the Lord God has led away from time to time from the house of Israel, according to his will and pleasure.[75]

And so it happened that the twelve tribes, once united under the proud banner of Israel, now became a people essentially without a name, itinerant groups uprooted from their homeland and displaced to many different parts of the world. No longer was there an area containing a numerous and significant population that could be regarded politically as Israelite. It was as though a people had been completely erased and others taken their place. Consequently, the phenomenon known as the scattering of Israel now reached its highest point, and during the centuries to follow it would continue, at the same time being supplemented by many intermarriages along the way as well as by people of Israelite lineage coming in from the premortal life!

The Gathering of Israel

Although the House of Israel was dispersed and scattered among the nations, there was also the promise that someday it would be gathered again. At some future time during the latter days, when the earth's regular history began drawing to a close, the Israelite people would start to be reunited, eventually being restored to their designated lands of inheritance.

All of this would be dependent, of course, upon the willingness of people to be gathered. Undoubtedly there would be those who would choose to go one way while others would go another. But the promise of a reunion or gathering had definitely been given, and one day it would be fulfilled.

The important question was how the gathering process would take place. In what way, for example, would an organization as vast and complex as the House of Israel be gathered together and united as a group? What kind of procedure or system of logistics would be involved?

There are obviously no simple answers to such a question, but one thing, at least, appears to be true, and that it is that the gathering of Israel was intended mainly to be a spiritual process as well as one that was physical and geographical. It would be meaningless, in other words, to gather people together in accordance with biblical prophecy unless there was some highly religious reason for doing so.

Surely it is a modern miracle that so many of the Jewish people have already made the exodus to Palestine during the last fifty years. Such an event undoubtedly fulfills part of what has been predicted in the Bible pertaining to the gathering of Israel. And yet the Jewish phenomenon represents only one or two of the tribes and also might be regarded more as a geographical event rather than one which is spiritual. This is especially true when considered from a Christian viewpoint.

The gathering spoken of in the Bible, in fact, was meant from the beginning to be initiated by one person, and one person only, namely the Lord Jesus Christ. He is, and always has been, the leading figure in the administration of the House of Israel, the president, as it were, through whom all things in that organization are to be accomplished.

He was the one in premortal life, under the direction of his Father, who set up the lineages of people transferring to earth and also "divided to the nations their inheritance." It was he who was Jehovah of the Old Testament and the promised Messiah of the New Testament. And in connection with all that has taken place, he was also the one who designed the grand operation known as the gathering of Israel which someday was to assemble all members of the Israelite family who obey certain laws and commandments and accept Jesus Christ as their leader.

This scheduled gathering would be the time in history when a certain stratum of people would be established, one destined to become like the city of Enoch. It would be an Israelite commonwealth, as it were, which would grow and progress until it finally realized its potential of being a holy nation, a peculiar treasure, and a kingdom of priests. Indeed, it would eventually expand into an entirely new kind of society that would become a light and beacon to the entire world.

The actual purpose of the gathering, therefore, would be to reconstruct the House of Israel, to assemble the different pieces and parts which had been scattered in many directions and put them back together again. It would be a process of reestablishing a condition that had existed earlier in premortal life. And yet in accomplishing this, the procedures involved would be very unlike those which might be expected.

They would not deal with large numbers of people at a time, but would be more likely to employ the craft of a fisherman or hunter who carefully and systematically searches out his prey. It would be a matter of finding those individuals who were of a particular religious nature and who were willing to be gathered, people who would join a common group one by one, by pairs, and by larger groups and families.

Behold, I will send for many fishers, saith the Lord, and they shall fish them; and after will I send for many hunters, and they shall hunt them from every mountain, and from every hill, and out of the holes of the rocks.[76]

Ideally, such a gathering would create a very controlled environment where people could focus more easily on things pertaining to spirituality and more effectively help carry out heaven's plan. It would give them the same opportunity their ancestors had in ancient times, namely that of participating in sacred ordinances and covenants and again bearing the name of Israel. This would be their inheritance from an Israelite ancestry and would make them charter members, so to speak, of what eventually would become a reunited House of Israel.

Yet in addition to this, one more circumstance would characterize such a gathering as a unique and unusual process, one main factor that was present from the beginning but for centuries had remained in the background. And that is that one of the tribes would now emerge as the leader in Israelite affairs, becoming the dominant influence in the gathering of Israel and occupying an inherited position of authority and leadership.

Ephraim, who had always been the junior member among tribal leaders and yet for some reason had been advanced to the firstborn position of birthright, would finally take over the earthly administration of the House of Israel, in whose care it would then continue. It would be Ephraim, in fact, who would be the primary force in assembling the Israelite people and again establishing them as a united group and kingdom.

All of this would be accomplished by his modern descendants acting under the calling and authority of their distant ancestor. Indeed, they would be his namesakes, carrying out a predetermined plan by way of the birthright and conducting the overall program for the restoration of Israel. It would be mainly through them that the affairs of the gathering would be planned and administered.

In the final stages, however, it would be both Ephraim and Manasseh, the two sons of Joseph, who would be in the forefront. The posterity of these two men together would be the ones to promote the strategic gathering of Israel as it prepared to enter the thousand year period known as the Millennium. It would be under their direction that a patriarchal blessing given to their father long ago would be fulfilled.

> His glory is like the firstling of his bullock, and his horns are like the horns of unicorns: with them he shall push the people together to the ends of the earth: and they are the ten thousands of Ephraim, and they are the thousands of Manasseh.[77]

These two brothers, represented by a numerous posterity, would be the principal figures in the gathering of the House of Israel. Although Ephraim would be the primary force, it would be through a joint administration of the brothers, acting under the direction of the Lord Jesus Christ, that all worthy descendants of Jacob would eventually be reunited. In an ultramodern world, they would then establish a new society called Zion, a counterpart of the ancient city of Enoch, and in company with that elite group finally enter the Millennium!

Part Three

A Latter-day Interlude

An Important Theory

In the latter days, after the House of Israel had been divided and scattered for hundreds of years, the time for the long-predicted gathering finally arrived. World conditions and historical events coincided to provide an opportune time for this important phenomenon to occur.

Descriptions of what happened, however, or when and where such a thing ever took place, are undoubtedly matters of opinion. As with other religious phenomena, there are many different theories and explanations. But the one which potentially is most valid, which outlines very systematically what the gathering of Israel is really about, is one that originated in a very miraculous and supernatural way.

It is a theory associated with a variety of circumstances that from the beginning might cause it to be more unlikely than any other explanation. Because of the type of occurrences involved, it is understandably something that is often difficult to believe. And yet without the information contained in this particular theory, very little might be known today about the concept of an Israelite gathering, and especially about anything pertaining to three separate Houses of Israel.

No other theory, in fact, suggests any kind of second or third house at all, and aside from the theory, a definition for the term Israelite is also open to question. Consequently, it is left to this lone explanation to provide the details of the historic gathering of Israel and the many important events which are to follow.

The story of how it all came about, an account even more miraculous than the gathering itself, originated in a remote backwoods area of North America during the early part of the nineteenth century.

The Sacred Records

In the year 1820 in the western part of New York state, an unusual event took place that was to have a marked effect upon many people in the world. A man named Joseph Smith found a set of metal plates filled with ancient engravings, and when deciphered and translated they claimed to be a history of some of the early inhabitants on the American continent.

Among other things, the plates contained numerous references to the House of Israel and described the migration of two Israelite groups from the Old World, as well as a third group basically of the same origin. Much of the content was highly religious in nature and often referred to the ministry of Jesus Christ, including a visit which he made to the people in the western hemisphere following his death and resurrection.

The record was eventually published, and because the ancient historian who prepared the plates in the beginning was named Mormon, the resulting book was called the *Book of Mormon*.

In addition to the account taken from the metal plates, Joseph Smith also published another book which today is called *The Doctrine and Covenants*. This included revelations which he received pertaining to religious matters, as well as to a series of events predicted for the last days. The circumstances surrounding both of these records were extremely different, even supernatural at times, and as a consequence their validity has often been called into question.

It is only through them, however, that a continuing story of the House of Israel can be told, since otherwise there is a serious lack of information. It is these two accounts, in fact, which state that the famous house of Jacob consisting of twelve tribes is still in existence and will definitely continue into the Millennium, as well as throughout the nebulous period to follow.

Yet in the mind of a reader, the validity of such records

depends heavily upon the status and reputation of the author, or in this case the man who brought the accounts to light. Before reading and considering any author's works, people naturally want to know about his credentials.

And in regard to Joseph Smith this is especially true, since the events and circumstances surrounding his lifetime, almost from the beginning, were highly irregular and out of the ordinary. Indeed, many of the things which he said happened to him are very hard for people to believe. A few weeks before his death, in fact, Joseph said on one occasion that if he had not personally experienced all that had occurred, he himself would not have believed it!

But a description of what took place, although still relatively unknown, does exist, and an acceptance or rejection of it is an important factor in any consideration of a third House of Israel.

A Night Visitor

The discovery of metal plates by Joseph Smith was no accident. He said that he learned of their existence from a man named Moroni who visited him one night during the early fall of 1823. It was not an ordinary visit, however, like someone might normally expect, but rather one that was related to the supernatural.

Still such an occurrence was not a total surprise to Joseph himself, whose life up to that point had been characterized by several remarkable experiences. Although not quite eighteen years of age at the time, he appeared to be set apart for a very different kind of destiny. His inclination was toward things that were religious and spiritual, and on the evening that he met his unusual visitor, he was saying a prayer in his room.

> While I was thus in the act of calling upon God, I discovered a light appearing in my room, which continued to increase until the room was lighter than at noonday, when immediately a personage appeared at my bedside, standing in the air, for his feet did not touch the floor.
>
> He had on a loose robe of most exquisite whiteness. It was a whiteness beyond anything earthly I had ever seen; nor do I believe that any earthly thing could be made to appear so exceedingly white and brilliant.
>
> Not only was his robe exceedingly white, but his whole person was glorious beyond description, and his countenance truly like lightning. The room was exceedingly light, but not so very bright as immediately around his person. When I first looked upon him, I was afraid; but the fear soon left me.
>
> He called me by name, and said unto me that he was a messenger sent from the presence of God to me, and that his name was Moroni; that God had a work for me to do, and that my name should be had for good and evil among all nations,

kindreds and tongues, or that it should be both good and evil spoken of among all people.

He said there was a book deposited, written upon gold plates, giving an account of the former inhabitants of this continent, and the source from whence they sprang. He also said that the fulness of the everlasting gospel was contained in it, as delivered by the Savior to the ancient inhabitants.

Also there were two stones in silver bows—and these stones, fastened to a breastplate, constituted what is called the Urim and Thummim—deposited with the plates; and the possession and use of these stones were what constituted Seers in ancient or former times; and God had prepared them for the purpose of translating the book.[78]

In this manner, Joseph Smith described the event which he said took place on the night of September 21, 1823. It is the explanation that he gave as to how he first learned about the metal plates, which eventually resulted in the translation of the Book of Mormon. And in reading such a miraculous account, it is not difficult to see why many people in modern society would find it hard to believe.

In any case, Joseph continued his account, telling how on the following day he went to a nearby hill which had been described to him as the place where the plates were buried.

And owing to the distinctness of the vision, which I had had concerning it, I knew the place the instant that I arrived there.

On the west side of this hill, not far from the top, under a stone of considerable size, lay the plates, deposited in a stone box. This stone was thick and rounding in the middle on the upper side, and thinner towards the edges, so that the middle part of it was visible above the ground, but the edge all around was covered with earth.

Having removed the earth, I obtained a lever, which I got fixed under the edge of the stone, and with a little exertion raised it up. I looked in, and there indeed did I behold the plates, the Urim and Thummim, and the breastplate, as stated by the messenger. The box in which they lay was formed by laying stones together in some kind of cement. In the bottom of the box were laid two stones crossways of the box, and on these stones lay the plates and other things with them.[79]

Once again, to read such an account, especially in today's modern world and culture, and to believe it could actually happen, might at first seem overwhelming. Certainly it requires faith as well as intellect. But at least such is Joseph Smith's story, and it forms one of the main bases for anything further that might be said concerning the three Houses of Israel.

Also it requires a conscientious decision on the part of a reader, or whoever might hear the story, as to whether or not the story is true. Unless some degree of credibility is given to what Joseph said, in other words, an account pertaining to Israelites in the present, and especially in the coming Millennium and the hereafter, might sometimes appear irrelevant and out of context.

The same is equally true with two other important events which occurred during this same time period: the restoration of the Aaronic Priesthood and the publication of the Doctrine and Covenants.

The Priesthood and a Book

Throughout Joseph Smith's brief lifetime, he experienced a great deal of adversity. As the messenger told him during his visit that night, his name would be both good and evil spoken of among all people. Yet despite the troubled times, he had many remarkable and miraculous experiences, which he often ascribed to *divine revelation* and the *ministering of angels*.

Some of these occurrences involved additional conversations with the angel Moroni, as well as a number of other individuals. Also on occasion, the events took place while he was in company with a man named Oliver Cowdery, a second witness, as it were, and his assistant in the translation of the metal plates.

It was in the spring of 1829 that these two men participated in an event that again was extremely unusual and out of the ordinary. It occurred while they were saying a prayer one day, asking for information about something recorded in the Book of Mormon. As they later recalled, the subject was in connection with baptism and the remission of sins.

> While we were thus employed, praying and calling upon the Lord, a messenger from heaven descended in a cloud of light, and having laid his hands on us, he ordained us, saying: *Upon you my fellow servants, in the name of Messiah, I confer the Priesthood of Aaron, which holds the keys of the ministering of angels, and of the gospel of repentance, and of baptism by immersion for the remission of sins; and this shall never be taken again from the earth until the sons of Levi do offer again an offering unto the Lord in righteousness.*

The one who reportedly spoke to Joseph and Oliver on this occasion said that his name was John, the same that is called John the Baptist in the New Testament. He told them he was acting under the direction of the ancient apostles Peter, James, and John. Certainly it was an unusual occurrence, especially for

Oliver Cowdery, and at the end of the messenger's visit, according to his instructions, the two men went to a nearby river and baptized one another by way of the authority they had just received.

Sometime later, Joseph Smith remarked,

> I baptized him first, and afterwards he baptized me, after which I laid my hands upon his head and ordained him to the Aaronic Priesthood, and afterwards he laid his hands on me and ordained me to the same priesthood, for so we were commanded.[80]

It was the type of thing that Joseph Smith himself admitted would have been difficult to believe, had he not experienced it personally. But it did happen, he said, and the event was confirmed by Oliver Cowdery.

The same kind of situation existed in still another important event that in some ways was no less miraculous, namely the publication of the book called The Doctrine and Covenants. This was an accumulation of written material on a wide variety of religious subjects, among which were several references to the House of Israel. And along with the Book of Mormon it consti- tuted an extremely valuable source of information.

Yet the book was much more than a collection of writings or a notable source of reference. In fact, if it is actually what it claims to be, it stands today as a series of divine revelations given to Joseph Smith by way of his calling as a prophet, and as such is intended for all people. Ultimately it is for all of those who accept the story about Moroni and the metal plates, as well as that of John and the Aaronic Priesthood.

In essence it also presents the idea that there is such a thing as prophets, revelation, and the ministering of angels. It is a message that the world's history is rapidly drawing to a close and that miraculous things are taking place, all in preparation for the Second Coming of Jesus Christ and the ushering in of the Millennium. Moreover, it is a sign and signal that the historic House of Israel, after an untold number of years, is now entering a new stage of existence, during which all of Israel's twelve tribes will again be reunited!

The Concept of Gathering

As a result of information given in the Doctrine and Covenants, Joseph Smith received authority and instructions to organize a church called *The Church of Jesus Christ of Latter-Day Saints*. The new organization was not a protestant group but rather, as its name implies, one that had existed previously and was now being restored in the latter days. And among its presiding officers was a prophet or president, along with a quorum of twelve apostles.

The Church was formed during the early part of 1830, and because of the Book of Mormon, it also became known as the Mormon Church. Endorsing as it did the idea of angels and divine revelation, it differed markedly from other religious groups and consequently entered upon a long history of public opposition and persecution. People were very suspicious of the new sect, not only religiously but politically as well, and as a result there were many probing questions.

On one occasion, for example, Joseph Smith was asked by a newspaper editor to state some of the tenets of Mormonism, and in response he submitted thirteen basic beliefs called The Articles of Faith. These covered a variety of church principles and doctrine, one of which was especially significant since it related to the gathering of the House of Israel. Moreover, it contained an important reference to the coming Millennium.

> We believe in the literal gathering of Israel, and in the restoration of the Ten Tribes; that Zion will be built upon this [the American] continent; that Christ will reign personally upon the earth; and that the earth will be renewed and receive its paradisiacal glory.[81]

The designation of Zion, according to the Doctrine and Covenants, referred to a special city to be built in the central part of the United States prior to the Millennium. It is here that the ten tribes will come, following their long seclusion in a place relative to the north country, to be crowned with glory by a people known as the *children of Ephraim*. In addition, the city will be one of the scenes of the Second Coming of Jesus Christ, during which time miraculous changes will take place throughout the earth.

Accompanying these occurrences will be the continuation of the gathering of Israel. The event which has been predicted by prophets down through the centuries will be in full operation. It was soon after the restoration of the Priesthood, in fact, according to Joseph Smith, that this worldwide movement formally began, the occasion being accompanied by another supernatural visitation.

Joseph said that during the early part of 1836, a man came to him and Oliver Cowdery and committed unto them "the keys of the gathering of Israel from the four parts of the earth, and the leading of the ten tribes from the land of the north." Authority was given to them at that time to rebuild the Israelite common-wealth, as it were, and in doing so commence a program outlined in ancient prophecy.

During this same time period, they also obtained information as to who the Israelites actually were and how they were to be gathered. Even though the Bible and Book of Mormon both contained numerous references to a latter-day gathering, it apparently was unknown in the beginning as to how it should be done. The necessary instructions, however, eventually came through revelation.

Joseph Smith learned that people of Israelite lineage were indeed scattered throughout the world but that the gathering itself was much more than merely finding them and bringing them together. Rather it would be a gradual process of searching for those who were amenable to a specific concept or idea pertaining to religion and were willing to be gathered as a group, people who believed in the ministering of angels and a restored gospel, for example, and who agreed to obey certain rules and commandments. It was set forth as a program designed and foreordained in heaven and delivered by way of divine revelation to the earth, a process not unlike that in former times.

When the program was eventually put into operation, it resulted in a small group of people who became the initial members of a restored church, an organization which continued to grow rapidly. It was also the beginning of the predicted gathering. Most of those involved were literally of Israelite lineage to begin with, as determined by genealogical research or a church blessing, yet in modern times it was necessary for them to be readmitted into the House of Israel through the ordinance of baptism. Also those who were not Israelite by birth were adopted into the lineage the same way.

So it was, therefore, through the instrumentality of Joseph Smith, who claimed as his authority the visitation and ministering of angels, that an entirely new type of religious activity began, one claiming additional scripture, a restored church, and the implementation of something that for most people was very unexpected, namely the appearance of a worldwide proselyting and recovery program and the formal announcement of the historic gathering of Israel!

A New Dispensation

As people started coming into the new church, one by one and by pairs and families, they theoretically were not just members of a religious sect or organization, but bonafide members of the House of Israel. By way of information contained in new scripture and the teachings of Joseph Smith, their Israelite lineage was now considered as valid as that pertaining to the Jewish faith or any other group who claimed Israelite ancestry.

According to new revelation, in fact, their own claim contained additional validity, not only through a belief in Jesus Christ but also because of a willingness to be gathered and to be counted among those who believed in a latter-day restoration of the gospel.

There was also the doctrine that the world had entered a new period of religious history called the Dispensation of the Fulness of Times. This was a concept involving six other such periods, namely those presided over formerly by Adam, Enoch, Noah, Abraham, Moses, and Jesus Christ. Now a seventh and final dispensation was taking place, one that would immediately precede the Millennium.

It was the idea that by way of the gathering, a certain type of society was being developed on earth in preparation for the Lord and his Second Coming, a group of people which had as their prototype the city of Enoch, as well as a relationship to the original group of Israelites in the premortal life. Moreover, as strongly suggested by the new religion, there was a second factor, something even more significant in an ultimate sense. And this was that after six thousand years of world history, this last dispensation of time would be a final consummation of world events, a grand finale, as it were, including not only a restoration of the gospel and the predicted gathering, but also the recognition of a third House of Israel which already was in progress!

Part Four

The Third House
of Israel

A Kingdom of Glory

Very little is known about a third House of Israel and when it began. In fact, seldom is reference ever made to a first house, much less a third. But three separate entities do exist, in a sense, each pertaining to an entirely different set of circumstances, and together they present a grand overview of man's progress from premortal life to earth life, and from there to the life hereafter.

Yet as to when a third house actually commenced, that is only speculation, although it would be logical to assume that it took place at the time of the Lord's resurrection and that he was its first member. All of those who were resurrected with him at that time would have become new members as well.

Soon after Jesus emerged from the tomb, a host of people who were buried in the Jerusalem area came out of their graves and appeared to many in the holy city. The Book of Mormon states that the same thing occurred among some of the ancient inhabitants living on the American continent.

In addition, according to the Doctrine and Covenants, all of the righteous dead who lived between the time of Adam and the time that Jesus was resurrected also came forth on this occasion. It was the beginning of the first resurrection, a process that would continue in the centuries which lay ahead.

Although only a few people are known to have actually been resurrected during this later time period, the prediction in the Bible is that another mass resurrection will take place at the time of the Lord's Second Coming. On the day that he appears in "the clouds of heaven with power and great glory," a large host of righteous dead will come forth from their graves and be caught up to meet him.

In view of these events, therefore, many people will have been resurrected by the time of the Lord's return and when the Millennium begins. The number of people will undoubtedly be small in comparison with the earth's total population, from the past to the present, yet it will still constitute a significant minority, one comprising the prestigious membership of the third House of Israel.

These people are also those who presently reside in the Kingdom of Heaven, having led righteous lives and complied with the necessary rules and commandments. For them the time of resurrection was a day of judgment and reward, permitting entrance into the highest kingdom of glory.

This higher kingdom, by way of definition, is outlined very specifically in the Doctrine and Covenants. In a lengthy discourse on things pertaining to life in the hereafter, it is referred to as an exclusive area or region that is termed celestial. The term refers to something more, however, than just a heavenly place. Rather it designates a level of high spiritual attainment and a specific degree of glory.

The same term also appears briefly in the book of First Corinthians in the Bible where it mentions the different kinds of resurrected bodies. No exact definition is given for it, but there is nevertheless a definite reference to the highest level of glory comparable to the sun.

> All flesh is not the same flesh, but there is one kind of flesh of men, another flesh of beasts, another of fishes, and another of birds. There are also celestial bodies, and bodies terrestrial: but the glory of the celestial is one, and the glory of the terrestrial is another.
>
> There is one glory of the sun, and another glory of the moon, and another glory of the stars: for one star differeth from another star in glory. So also is the resurrection of the dead.[82]

This means that there are two main types of glory characterizing the resurrection of the dead, namely the celestial and also the terrestrial, symbolized respectively by the sun and the moon. Along with these a third one is implied which has as its symbol the stars. But still there is no biblical explanation of what the celestial or the other two glories actually entail, and it is left to the Doctrine and Covenants, once again, to give additional information.

In the 76th section of that record, there is a detailed description of the third or highest degree of glory, the place known as the Celestial Kingdom. It is a commentary on those who reside there, and the last part especially presents an unusual view.

> These shall dwell in the presence of God and his Christ forever and ever,
>
> These are they whom he shall bring with him when he shall come in the clouds of heaven to reign on the earth over his people.
>
> These are they who shall have part in the first resurrection. These are they who shall come forth in the resurrection of the just.
>
> These are they who are come unto Mount Zion, and unto the city of the living God, the heavenly place, the holiest of all.
>
> These are they who have come to an innumerable company of angels, to the general assembly and church of Enoch, and of the Firstborn. These are they whose names are written in heaven, where God and Christ are the judge of all.
>
> These are they whose bodies are celestial, whose glory is that of the sun, even the glory of God, the highest of all, whose glory the sun of the firmament is written of as being typical.[83]

Then finally, after all of this, these people are also the so-called children of promise and of the covenant, either by way of actual heredity or through the process of adoption. As the progeny of Abraham, Isaac and Jacob and the earlier patriarchs before them, they are those who were faithful and obedient during life on earth and showed a willingness to be gathered. They are those who carried out heaven's plan. And because of this accomplishment, which represents an important period of testing and qualification, they now possess a permanent Israelite citizenship in the association of the third House of Israel.

High Cost of Entry

Along with the Celestial Kingdom, symbolized by the glory of the sun, the Doctrine and Covenants also describes the kingdoms known as *Terrestrial* and *Telestial*, represented respectively by the moon and the stars. And although all three of these areas together are what generally might be called *Heaven*, the last two are not the places where God dwells. They also have no Israelite connection.

Only in the Celestial Kingdom, according to the revelations, can people attain to the highest quality of life in the hereafter. In this kingdom only is there a level of spirituality which permits an association in the presence of God.

This latter environment is much like that of the Garden of Eden and the city of Enoch or of that in the premortal life. It is characterized by the type of lifestyle that might well be regarded as paradisiacal or utopian, a condition which consequently makes the cost of entry necessarily high. And yet what it amounts to in essence is nothing more than being qualified for membership in the third House of Israel.

It is the requirement that a person live a good life, one that is celestial in nature, and then further qualifying by believing in Jesus Christ and obeying the principles and ordinances of the gospel. Essentially it means that he or she must develop a certain type of body or personality, again, one that is celestial, which will be compatible with the kingdom and glory of God.

> For he who is not able to abide the law of a celestial kingdom cannot abide a celestial glory.[84]

It is also the concept and idea that only those people who have suitably prepared themselves for the highest kingdom will feel comfortable when they get there. For them it will be a natural setting and environment in which to continue an eternal progression.

The other two kingdoms, the Terrestrial and Telestial, are

also places of glory, but less important in terms of lifestyle and spiritual accomplishment. As described in the Doctrine and Covenants, these are areas which will be inhabited by people who were not as faithful in carrying out the plan of heaven and as a result will inherit a lesser reward. Yet in regard to the glory involved, including living conditions and sociality, the record states that both will be of such a nature that surpasses all human understanding.

At the same time there is no question but what the Celestial Kingdom is what mankind should idealistically desire, the glory compared to that of the sun as described in the Bible, and one also which is mentioned briefly by the Apostle Paul as a third heaven.[85] This is the glory that prophets throughout history have referred to as a place of paradise and the kingdom of God.

Certainly it is also the supreme ideal established in the beginning, that which represents the highest level of achievement during premortal life and earth life, as well as the final goal and destination of all who belong to the House of Israel!

Steps Toward Salvation

Entrance into the Celestial Kingdom, as outlined in the Doctrine and Covenants and other revelations attributed to Joseph Smith, is generally obtained by way of three basic steps: (1) leading a good life and developing a celestial body and personality, (2) obeying certain rules and commandments, including baptism and a willingness to be gathered, and (3) obtaining a celestialized resurrected body. The second step includes temple attendance for the purpose of receiving the higher religious ordinances.

All of these are very important, and in connection with the Celestial Kingdom, they qualify a person for membership in the third House of Israel!

And yet the most vital step of all is undoubtedly the one that pertains to a good life and a celestial body. Regardless of a person's lineage, and whether or not he or she knows about the plan of salvation, none of these things will be of any value in a celestial sense if unaccompanied by righteous living.

Aside from church membership, or other kinds of religious affiliation, it is a celestial type of being or personality which must be developed in order to qualify for the highest kingdom. After that is accomplished, other requirements can usually be taken care of in due time, either while a person is alive or following death and entrance into the Spirit World.

One of the unusual practices in The Church of Jesus Christ of Latter-day Saints, in fact, which again is mentioned in the Doctrine and Covenants, is temple work for the dead as well as for the living. If a worthy person dies without meeting the basic requirements for salvation, a worthy member of the Church can go to a temple in his or her behalf and do what work is necessary. Baptism for the dead, marriage for eternity, and the endowment are all examples of temple ordinances that can be performed in this way.

The important thing is to lead a good life. If people possess a celestial spirit and personality, and do not have ample opportunity to do temple work for themselves while living, it is presumed that in the hereafter they will normally accept the work which is done for them vicariously. Otherwise, different circumstances will prevail.

The vital question always remains as to what level of humanity and spirituality a person can acquire during a lifetime. If it is celestial, and other qualifications are met, he or she most likely will inherit a celestial kingdom and glory. If not, except in very few cases, it will be a kingdom that is terrestrial or telestial. One thing is certain, however, and that is that according to the plan established in heaven, it is definitely the glory of the sun, and not that of the moon or stars, to which men and women should aspire!

Concept of the Temple

If there is one main idea in Mormon theology that symbolizes the Celestial Kingdom, other than the glory of the sun, it is undoubtedly the idea of temples. These are places where specific instructions and ceremonies take place which theoretically qualify a person for entrance into the highest kingdom in heaven. By way of baptisms, confirmations, washings, annointings, endowments and sealings, people attend to the business of personal and family salvation, as well as proxy work for those who are dead.

Temples are also an important aspect of the gathering of Israel. Certainly one of the most important teachings of Joseph Smith was that the purpose of the gathering, in the first place, was not only to draw people together for instruction and edification but "to build unto the Lord a house" in which to administer and receive sacred ordinances, both for the living and for the dead.

In regard to baptism for the dead, for example, each time that someone is baptized in the temple and given the gift of the Holy Ghost for a person who has died, and that person accepts it in the hereafter, it means that one new member has been added to the House of Israel. The same is also true of work performed for the living outside the temple. Whenever someone obeys the necessary rules and commandments, including baptism and the ordinances that follow, he or she officially becomes an Israelite, and again there is an increase in membership.

The ordinances of baptism, therefore, and receiving the gift of the Holy Ghost actually become the preliminary entrance and gateway into the Celestial Kingdom, which is exactly the same thing that Jesus taught. "Except a man be born of the water and of the spirit" he said, "he cannot enter the kingdom of heaven."[86]

And yet according to Mormon philosophy, only one type of baptism, both for the living and for the dead, is acceptable, and

116

that is baptism by immersion and by the authority that was restored by an angel. When the messenger conferred the priesthood upon Joseph Smith and Oliver Cowdery that day, it was then that the ordinance of baptism in modern times again became valid. And since then it has been used exclusively as the preliminary ordinance in connection with salvation and is an important instrument in the gathering and reconstruction of the House of Israel.

Along with baptism, however, and receiving the gift of the Holy Ghost, there are additional ordinances that must be received in order to obtain full benefits in the Celestial Kingdom. These are those which usually can be performed only within temples. Washings and annointings, followed by the ordinance known as the endowment, are all designed to bring a person to the very threshold of heaven itself. Just as the high priest in ancient Israel entered the tabernacle and approached the veil, establishing a personal relationship with the Lord, so can a worthy person in a temple today do essentially the same thing.

The endowment, in fact, as it has been defined, is to receive all those ordinances in the House of the Lord that will enable a person to make a transition from earth life to the hereafter. Symbolically, it represents walking "back to the presence of the Father, passing the angels who stand as sentinels, being enabled to give them the key words, the signs and tokens, pertaining to the Holy Priesthood," and eventually gaining eternal life and exaltation, all of which can be accomplished within the walls of a temple![87]

In addition to this, however, there is one last ordinance and ceremony that needs to be accomplished in order to qualify for a final benefit, one pertaining to what is called sealings. Before a person qualifies for the highest level in the Celestial Kingdom, he or she must be married and sealed within a temple, not just for time but also for eternity, following which all of their children, if they have any, can then be bonded to them by authority of the Priesthood. For married people who die without being sealed, this can be done vicariously in temples.

It is this last ordinance that represents the ideal goal and destiny within The Church of Jesus Christ of Latter-day Saints. It is the crowning point in what has become known as the plan of salvation relating to the Celestial Kingdom and the House of Israel. It is not a plan designed by man, according to Joseph Smith, nor one brought forth by any human hand, but rather a plan revealed from heaven through the ministration of angels.

By way of messengers such as Moroni and John the Baptist, as well as others, it is the authority restored to earth during the Dispensation of the Fulness of Times whereby mankind can attain to the highest kingdom in the hereafter, not one comparable to the moon or stars, but that which was prepared from the beginning for those who are true and faithful and whose circumstances pertain to a celestial glory and the brightness and glory of the sun.

Restoration of Truth

One of the main concepts that Joseph Smith taught during his lifetime, a principle related to the three kingdoms of glory, was that God is not just a spirit or force throughout the universe but a resurrected being with a body of flesh and bones. He is all knowing and all powerful, a glorified person who can physically appear to men on earth when necessary and talk with them face to face. This turned out to be a very different idea and naturally contradicted many sectarian beliefs.

On one occasion Joseph said,

> If the veil were rent today, and the great God who holds this world in its orbit, and who upholds all worlds and all things by his power, were to make himself visible, I say if you were to see him today, you would see him like a man in form, like yourselves in all the person, image, and very form as a man.[88]

In connection with this concept, a similar teaching pertained to the place where God lives, or the site of the Celestial Kingdom. As recorded in the Doctrine and Covenants, the supreme ruler of the universe resides on a globe or planet which is likened symbolically to a sea of glass and fire. It is a place inhabited by celestial beings and an innumerable company of angels. Moreover, according to additional revelation, it is in a different situation from earth, possessing a different time reckoning and lying in the vicinity of a secondary planet named Kolob.[89]

Obviously these were revolutionary ideas during the time of Joseph Smith, and yet they are just two of many that were part of a restored gospel which he inaugurated. Through him the idea of revelation itself was reintroduced into world society, and many new concepts came into existence. It was as though the heavens were opened for a time in order for man's mind to be enlightened and his span of learning expanded.

Former principles and teachings were restored and new ones

introduced as religion took on a new meaning. No longer was there a separation between God and man like that which had developed through the ages, but by way of a restoration of truth, the veil of darkness was parted and the curtain of uncertainty withdrawn. At least so were the claims of a modern-day prophet.

The real meaning of Joseph Smith's mission, in fact, was established during a very early time period when he was only fourteen years of age. Before any of the visitations from resurrected beings such as Moroni and John ever took place, there was one other occurrence which was greater and more significant than them all. Indeed, it was this earlier event which theoretically set Joseph apart not as a sectarian minister or religious reformer but as one who opened a new dispensation of the gospel and who in doing so took his place among the prophets of old.

The event occurred in the western part of the state of New York during the year of 1820. According to his own story, Joseph Smith was just a young man at the time and yet very interested in religion, being caught up in some of the protestant revivals of the day that were being held near his home. His intent was to join a church, but because the various ministers differed so much in how they presented the gospel, creating confusion and strife, he said it was difficult for him to make a decision.

He continued to attend the various meetings, however, and was often troubled as to what he should do. His mind underwent what he called "serious reflection and great uneasiness." But he persisted in his search for truth, and the information which he finally obtained not only answered his question about church membership, but it gave him a new kind of insight into the personality of God, as well as a brief glimpse into the Celestial Kingdom itself.

> While I was laboring under the extreme difficulties caused by the contests of these parties of religionists, I was one day reading the Epistle of James, first chapter and fifth verse, which reads: *If any of you lack wisdom, let him ask of God*

that giveth to all men liberally and upbraideth not, and it shall be given him.

Never did any passage of scripture come with more power to the heart of man than this did at this time to mine. It seemed to enter with great force into every feeling of my heart. I reflected on it again and again, knowing that if any person needed wisdom from God, I did. For how to act I did not know, and unless I could get more wisdom than I then had, I would never know, for the teachers of religion of the different sects understood the same passages of scripture so differently as to destroy all confidence in settling the question by an appeal to the Bible.

At length I came to the conclusion that I must either remain in darkness and confusion, or else I must do as James directs, that is, ask of God. I at length came to the determination to 'ask of God,' concluding that if he gave wisdom to them that lacked wisdom, and would give liberally and not upbraid, I might venture.

So in accordance with this, my determination to ask of God, I retired to the woods to make the attempt. It was on the morning of a beautiful clear day, early in the spring of eighteen hundred and twenty. It was the first time in my life that I had made such an attempt, for amidst all my anxieties I had never as yet made the attempt to pray vocally.

After I had retired to the place where I had previously designed to go, having looked around me and finding myself alone, I kneeled down and began to offer up the desire of my heart to God. I had scarcely done so, when immediately I was seized upon by some power which entirely overcame me and had such an astonishing influence over me as to bind my tongue so that I could not speak. Thick darkness gathered around me, and it seemed to me for a time as if I were doomed to sudden destruction.

But exerting all my powers to call upon God to deliver me out of the power of this enemy which had seized upon me, and at the very moment when I was ready to sink into despair and abandon myself to destruction—not to an imaginary ruin, but to the power of some actual being from the unseen world who had such marvelous power as I had never before felt in any being—just at this moment of great alarm, I saw a pillar of light exactly over my head, above the brightness of the sun, which descended gradually until it fell upon me.

It no sooner appeared, than I found myself delivered from the enemy which held me bound. When the light rested upon me, I saw two personages, whose brightness and glory defy all description, standing above me in the air. One of them spake unto me, calling me by name, and said, pointing to the other— *This is My Beloved Son. Hear Him!*[90]

This one event, coming at the beginning of Joseph Smith's controversial career as a religious leader, proved to be the genesis of a multitude of new religious concepts. Certainly one of them was the idea that God the Father and his son Jesus Christ are two separate individuals, two resurrected human beings who have again appeared to a man on earth and talked with him as one person talks with another.

It was also the idea of restoration, the resumption of former religious practices and teachings which for one reason or another had been discontinued down through the centuries. During his remarkable experience in the woods, Joseph learned that he should join none of the existing churches but wait for a time in the future when he would be instrumental in establishing a new church, one that had been on the earth formerly and was now to be restored.

This meant that despite protestant improvements in a changing Christianity, the actual church which Jesus Christ organized in the Meridian of Time was not currently in existence upon the earth. The different religions in the modern world contained doctrines that had "a form of godliness but they denied the power thereof." Consequently, the conditions necessitated a restoration of the earlier church, complete with its organization, priesthood authority, and original doctrine and teachings. All of this was according to the testimony of Joseph Smith.

In addition to these circumstances, miraculous as they were, what happened in the woods that day was also a prelude to many other important events still to occur in the future, one in particular which had been pending for centuries. This was an event that had been predicted by prophets ever since the days following Egyptian bondage and was to be among the final occurrences before the Second Coming of Jesus Christ and the Millennium.

Now was the exact time in history for the phenomenon known as the gathering of Israel to take place, a movement that would promote not only a worldwide assemblage of people and introduce a new concept of religion but would also be part of an extraordinary climax and denouement of world affairs, including a continuing reference to the man known as Ephraim and also the return of the legendary lost tribes from a mysterious hiding place somewhere in relation to the north country.

Return of the Tribes

In very few places in scripture is there a subject as significant and mysterious as that of the ten lost tribes of Israel. To those who are acquainted with history, they have been a strange enigma since the time they first went into Assyrian captivity and later disappeared in the north country. For many centuries they have remained a mystery as to their geographical location and true identity.

The most prevalent theory is that as a people they are presently dispersed among the nations and will someday be part of the gathering of Israel that will be coming from the north. In addition, there is a variety of other views. Yet the particular theory or hypothesis that might be closest to the truth is one which says that the tribes are still a homogeneous group, isolated in some manner from the mainstream of society and waiting for the time when they will make their reappearance.

In spite of the mystery that surrounds them, for example, there are certain clues which suggest they have definitely remained together. One of these is found in the record taken from metal plates known as the Book of Mormon. In this account it tells about Jesus Christ visiting some of the early inhabitants of the American continent following his death and resurrection, some of the "other sheep" that he had spoken of earlier while still in Palestine.[91]

> And verily I say unto you, that ye are they of whom I said: Other sheep I have which are not of this fold; them also I must bring, and they shall hear my voice; and there shall be one fold and one shepherd.

He then spoke of additional tribes that were lost. "I have other sheep," he said, "which are not of this land, neither of the land of Jerusalem, neither in any part of that land round about where I have been to minister. For they of whom I speak are they who have not as yet heard my voice; neither have I at any time manifested myself unto them.

> But I have received a commandment of the Father that I shall go unto them, and they shall hear my voice, and shall be numbered among my sheep, that there may be one fold and one shepherd; therefore I go to show myself unto them.

So it was that on that occasion Jesus mentioned three distinct groups: the people in Palestine, those on the American Continent, and still others at some other location. The latter unmistakably referred to the tribes who were lost, and the description of them definitely suggested a separate and combined group. This also was implied in what Jesus told the people at the end of his visit.

> But now I go unto the Father, and also to show myself unto the lost tribes of Israel, for they are not lost unto the Father, for he knoweth whither he hath taken them.[92]

The events in question, occurred almost two thousand years ago, and much has happened since then. The Nephite civilization, as some of the people in America were called, became extinct in the 5th Century A.D., and it might be that the lost tribes in the meantime have also had a radical change of situation, such as being dispersed and intermingled among the nations.

But still there are further clues which imply that they are a united group and have stayed together, one of the most important being a brief description of their predicted return as recorded in the 133rd section of the Doctrine and Covenants. This is an account that some would interpret figuratively or symbolically, but a careful reading of the text suggests otherwise. Indeed, the miraculous things that are scheduled to happen in the future might very well be taken literally, occurring exactly as stated in the scripture.

> And they who are in the north countries shall come in remembrance before the Lord; and their prophets shall hear his voice and shall no longer stay themselves; and they shall smite the rocks, and the ice shall flow down at their presence. And an highway shall be cast up in the midst of the great deep.[93]

Like other such phenomenal occurrences, especially those mentioned in the Bible, the ones that will accompany the lost tribes as they make their dramatic return will be very much out of the ordinary. Certainly the idea of crumbling rock and falling ice, followed by a highway rising up out of the sea, creates a visual image that is not easy to comprehend, one also that suggests symbolism rather than realism. But the actual wording is there, and surrounding textual material is no less spectacular, all of which gives a strong indication that some kind of supernatural explanation is intended.

Just as the circumstances pertaining to the tribes have been different and unusual from the beginning, so also are the conditions of their return likely to be the same. Any other kind of situation might turn out to be too commonplace and generic. At this time in history particularly, when so many other miraculous things are taking place, it should be no surprise if the ten lost tribes of Israel reappear in exactly the same manner as described in the Doctrine and Covenants.

And when they do, according to the record, they will be led by prophets. It will be these individuals, in fact, who will smite the rocks, presumably causing ice to fall, after which the people will cross a large expanse of water by way of some type of highway. Then in fulfillment of prophecy, they will travel southward toward a city called Zion.

> And they shall bring forth their rich treasures unto the children of Ephraim, my servants,
>
> And the boundaries of the everlasting hills shall tremble at their presence.
>
> And there shall they fall down and be crowned with glory, even in Zion, by the hands of the servants of the Lord, even the children of Ephraim.
>
> And they shall be filled with songs of everlasting joy.
>
> Behold, this is the blessing of the everlasting God upon the tribes of Israel, and the richer blessing upon the head of Ephraim and his fellows.[94]

In that day it will be Ephraim, in a very real sense, receiving blessings from Ephraim, two groups of Israelites, both associated with the same progenitor and one group being acknowledged by the other. One will be the recipient of an important religious endowment, and the other the benefactor. It will be Ephraim of old being blessed by a kindred group, who likewise stems from Ephraim or in some cases has become a member of that lineage through adoption.

During pre-captivity days, the ten tribes were referred to as Ephraim as well as the Kingdom of Israel. This was partly because Ephraim in some ways was the most prominent tribe and sometimes would exert itself beyond the authority of the others. Such status was indicated by the Lord himself on one occasion when he alluded to what had taken place during the Assyrian conquests. Speaking to the tribes of Judah and Benjamin through the prophet Jeremiah, he said,

> And I will cast you out of my sight, as I have cast out all your brethren, even the whole seed of Ephraim.[95]

This particular tribe was important in former times, therefore, and will continue to be a dominate influence in the affairs of the House of Israel. Especially will this be true of those in the city of Zion who will be in charge of all aspects of the process of gathering. According to information given to Joseph Smith, members of this latter group will be the ones occupying the higher levels of the priesthood and possessing the important keys of authority. Yet among the lost tribes, there will undoubtedly be many in that society also who are literal descendants of Ephraim,   children by inheritance of the same name, and they very likely will be providing a similar type of leadership within their   own group.

In any case, it is another reminder of the importance which this one prestigious tribe has within the House of Israel. Out of all the tribes, this is the one that anciently acquired precedence over the others, possessing the birthright and also a designation of firstborn. Indeed, it is mainly the descendants of this one tribe who today are directing the entire operations of the gathering of Israel. And it will be this same tribal group, along with the descendants of Manasseh, who will build a brand new city called Zion and in that place be the welcoming committee, as it were, for the returning lost tribes when they finally emerge from their hiding place in the north countries.

The Doctrine and Covenants

The restoration of the ten tribes will not only be a significant event within itself but also a vital part of the larger gathering of Israel. It is unknown how many descendants of the original group will return, but at least it will be those who have obeyed certain rules and commandments and are willing to be gathered. Also the blessings which they will receive at the hands of the children of Ephraim, including the crowning with glory spoken of, will undoubtedly be temple-related, namely receiving the higher religious ordinances of personal and family salvation.

An account of what will happen, once again, is found in the 133rd section of the Doctrine and Covenants and is no less spectacular in some ways than other miraculous events described in the same section. It is just one of several occurrences pertaining to the end of the world and the personal appearances of Jesus Christ.

Sometime after the advent of the ten tribes, for example, or possibly sometime before, the Lord will appear at a variety of places on the earth's surface, initiating the event of his Second Coming. That which has been predicted all down through the centuries will become the crowning point of human history.

The record states,

> For behold, he shall stand upon the mount of Olivet, and upon the mighty ocean, even the great deep, and upon the islands of the sea, and upon the land of Zion.

> And he shall utter his voice out of Zion, and he shall speak from Jerusalem, and his voice shall be heard among all people. And it shall be a voice as the voice of many waters, and as the voice of a great thunder, which shall break down the mountains, and the valleys shall not be found.

> He shall command the great deep, and it shall be driven back into the north countries, and the islands shall become one land; and the land of Jerusalem and the land of Zion shall be

turned back into their own place, and the earth shall be like as it was in the days before it was divided.

And the Lord, even the Savior, shall stand in the midst of his people, and shall reign over all flesh.[96]

The description of these miraculous events, of course, including the return of the ten lost tribes, is found only in the book which has come to be known as the Doctrine and Covenants. In this record alone is there this type of scriptural account. Indeed, if it were not for this particular book containing the revelations of Joseph Smith, the details pertaining to these and other important occurrences would still be unknown.

But the book does exist, and according to the testimony of many people, it comes from a divine source and is regarded as scripture. For more than a hundred and fifty years it has been published in numerous languages and distributed throughout the world. And although its authenticity so far has been recognized by relatively few, its contents make it clear that the revelations given are for the benefit of all people.

Moreover, because the material in the 133rd section , as well as the 76th, has provided such important and unique information, not only regarding the ten tribes but also matters pertaining to the Celestial Kingdom, it gives additional credibility to other things which Joseph Smith taught during his lifetime. The boldness of the text and the tenor of its content both suggest that something beyond ordinary experience is present and that the man who said he obtained new knowledge through divine revelation was in reality telling the truth. There is much more to the Doctrine and Covenants, in other words, than just an important religious document.

And when the day comes that all of this is confirmed, then will everyone know, as Isaiah and Ezekiel said of old, that "a marvelous work and a wonder" has been revealed to the people and that indeed "a prophet hath been among them!"[97]

Ephraim

Ephraim was his name, the son of Joseph and Asenath. He was the one in Israel who held the birthright and was designated as the firstborn.

He was born in Egypt long ago and by way of his parentage was one of the prestigious sons in the Egyptian Empire. His standing was that of prince or nobleman, the grandson of the Priest of On.

And yet his true significance as a person had nothing to do with the culture in which he lived, but rather with a lowly group of Hebrews who had settled nearby. Like Moses who followed after him, he was raised in a palace as a prince but more importantly was a descendant of Abraham and bore the name of Israel.

For hundreds of years after his death, his descendants perpetuated his name and lineage from Egypt to Palestine, through the well-known eras of exodus, judges and kings. They became one of the most important tribes and were a significant factor in the eventual division of the House of Israel. Many of them also were among the captives taken into Assyria and were part of those who became the ten lost tribes.

At that point in history, however, their identity as a group temporarily became extinct, as did that of most of the other tribes, and for centuries any kind of influence pertaining to Ephraim lay dormant. For a while, it was as though a former name and tradition had been completely erased.

But then came Joseph Smith at the beginning of the 19th Century who claimed new revelation and reintroduced not only the idea of Ephraim but along with it the concept of the entire gathering of Israel. It was the lineage of Ephraim, he said, under the direction of heaven, that was now to direct all operations in the latter days, eventually bringing the Israelite tribes together again and returning them to their original lands of inheritance. Also they would be the ones in the future who would receive the ten lost tribes in the city of Zion, crowning them with glory and bestowing upon them an important religious endowment.

The significance in all of this, of course, is the tremendous focus placed upon Ephraim. From the very beginning, at the time that Jacob laid his hands upon him and blessed him, setting him apart as the preferred son in Israel, he was marked for some unique and special purpose. The same was especially true when he was named the firstborn.

An indication of his importance, especially as a progenitor, was also expressed in the years that followed as his descendants became a strong influence among the ten tribes of the Kingdom of Israel. The tribes collectively, in fact, were sometimes referred to not as Israel, but only by his personal name of Ephraim.

But still it was not until the latter days, after the times of disruption and a long period of dormancy, that he eventually reached the high standing that Jacob of old had pronounced upon him. It was not until this one specific era of history that those who were heirs to his name finally came forward to fulfill their destiny and carry out the important work which anciently had been assigned to them.

Now was the time, in other words, for the Israelite people to be gathered, the time scheduled for the reconstruction of the House of Israel. According to Joseph Smith, this was the Dispensation of the Fulness of Times that was to precede the Second Coming of Jesus Christ and the Millennium. It was a highly strategic period in the world's history that had been predicted for centuries, and at the very center of operations were the descendants and representatives of one specific man: Ephraim, the son of Joseph and Asenath of Egypt and the second great-grandson of Abraham.

Indeed, members of the tribe of Ephraim are now the authority behind the entire movement of gathering and consequently in full charge of its administration, qualifying people in many different places of the world for an inheritance in the Celestial Kingdom and preparing them for membership in the third House of Israel!

Postscript

In retrospect, one of the important questions in Israelite history is why so many members of the House of Israel through the ages failed to carry out heaven's plan. Why were there those who had allegedly been faithful and obedient in premortal life but then chose the opposite kind of life once they transferred to earth?

Those people who were of high standing in pre-earth life would generally have been expected to do better than those who were not. Surely they should have been predisposed to accept the truth once they heard it, but apparently this did not always happen. In so many instances, the children of Israel were far from anything which would suggest that they had been more than ordinary or commonplace during a previous lifetime.

And so what is the answer? What explanation might be given to account for such discrepancy? If it is true that people are born on earth, both as to time and place, according to an earlier spiritual status, why was there such a lack of consistency among the Israelites in the way they sometimes conducted their lives? As members of this particular group, why were they not more faithful? Answers and opinions vary, of course, but two that might be mentioned once more are the following.

(1) One possible answer was voiced by the Apostle Paul in the New Testament when he said, "For they are not all Israel which are of Israel." [98] In other words, despite their success in the premortal life, many people later succumbed to negative forces and influences and consequently failed. Even though they were of Israelite lineage, they did not act that way once they came to earth. Supposedly they should have been more inclined toward righteousness because of their previous background and experience, but often this was not the case.

Such instances would include people who dropped from the highest to the lowest, such as a Saul or a Solomon, or any number of Israelite kings. Or it might be that many of those who failed belonged to one of the lower levels of Israelite society while in premortal life.

(2) By way of Paul's statement in the New Testament, however, and according to a different interpretation, another possibility is that people who sometimes ended up with severe problems on earth never belonged to the House of Israel in the first place, even though they were born into that lineage. For one reason or another, a certain mixing might have taken place from time to time where people from Israelite and non-Israelite groups were placed together.

Cain being born into the same family with Abel, for example, or rebellious Jews being placed among believing disciples during the time of Jesus would again suggest this kind of situation. Such a theory could avoid the idea that large numbers of people failed during earth life who had earlier gone through successful schooling and testing in premortal life.

Yet if it does turn out to be true that many are unsuccessful despite previous high standards, it presents a very stark reality, and that is that a great deal depends upon what people do with their lives once they transfer to earth, regardless of what they might have accomplished in an earlier lifetime. The time on earth might be relatively short, but the idea of a crucial period of final testing is definitely there.

There is also the suggestion and possibility that those who were not completely successful in premortal life can still turn their lives around on earth and possibly for the first time gain entrance into the Israelite family.

But one thing is certain. Through the interaction of divine mercy and justice, there will be no inequitable occurrences during future judgments! Everything will be administered in a fair and reasonable way. Examples might be that one person would not completely lose a high status acquired during a long premortal life because of certain negative actions during a brief lifetime on earth, and by the same reasoning, another would not be able to make too quick of a change from a relatively low status to one that is extremely high.

Obviously, when the final judgments take place, many different factors will be brought into play. On that occasion, difficult and troublesome problems will be solved and apparent discrepancies clarified. Many puzzling questions will be answered. And one of these, of course, will be why so many people in the lineages of Israel supposedly came to earth with an excellent record and good intentions, only to meet challenging circumstances and consequently fail. It is the continuing question as to why they did not live up to expectations.

And yet again there is always the possibility that such people were never of the House of Israel to begin with. At least a person might choose to think so.

References

Note: The King James Version of the Bible, The Book of Mormon, The Doctrine and Covenants, and The Pearl of Great Price are standard works of The Church of Jesus Christ of Latter-day Saints.

1. Exodus 19:5-6
2. Jeremiah 1:4-5
3. Abraham 3:23
4. Genesis 25:23
5. Genesis 48: 13-19
6. Jeremiah 31:9
7. John 17:5
8. John 8:26, 28
9. John 5:19-21
10. Romans 8 :29-30
11. Romans 9:10-12
12. Ephesians 1:3-6
13. Deuteronomy 32: 7-9
14. *The New English Bible with the Apocrypha* (New York: Oxford University Press, 1976), p 217; *The Septuagint Version of the Old Testament and Apocrypha* (London: Zondervan Publishing House, 1976), p 276
15. Acts 17:24-26
16. Romans 9:6-7
17. John 8:37, 39, 44, 47
18. John 10:14, 27, 29; 6:37
19. Revelation 12:3-4; Acts 17:26
20. Isaiah 14:12-13
21. Deuteronomy 32:8; Acts 17:26
22. Genesis 35:10
23. Genesis 48:18-19
24. 1 Chronicles 5:1
25. Jeremiah 31:9
26. Genesis 45:5,7
27. Exodus 12:37-38
28. Exodus 1:7, 9-12

29. Genesis 17:20; 25:13-16
30. Exodus 39:8, 10-14
31. Numbers 1:2-4, 16
32. Numbers 2:2-34; 3:12-38; 10:11-28
33. Numbers 13:17-20
34. Deuteronomy 9:6-7
35. Genesis 49:1-2
36. Genesis 49:26
37. Deuteronomy 33:17
38. Exodus 19:5-6
39. Joshua 4:2-3
40. Joshua 1:5, 9
41. Numbers 34:29
42. Joshua 17:14, 17-18
43. Judges 12:6
44. Judges 21:2-3
45. 1 Samuel 9:2
46. 1 Samuel 18:16
47. 2 Samuel 5:3-5; 3:10
48. 2 Samuel 24:9; 1 Chronicles 21:5
49. 1 Kings 4:20-21, 25
50. 2 Chronicles 9:23; 1 Kings 10: 6-8
51. 1 Kings 12:4
52. 1 Kings 12:14
53. 1 Kings 12:16
54. 2 Samuel 19:43; 20:1
55. 1 Kings 11:31, 36
56. 1 Kings 12:15, 24
57. 2 Chronicles 25:10
58. 2 Kings 14:13-14
59. 2 Kings 15:29; 1 Chronicles 5:26
60. H. R. Hall, *The Ancient history of the Near East* (London: Metheun & Co., Ltd., 1957), p 466. Others have also expressed this same view, pointing out that only a part of conquered area was taken into captivity.
61. 2 Kings 17:5-6
62. Andre Parrot, *Samaria, The Capital of the Kingdom of Israel* (New York: Philosophical Library, Inc., 1959), p 51. The number of captives usually mentioned in other texts, and the one that appears to be correct, is 27,290.

63. 2 Kings 17:23-24
64. Jeremiah 7:15
65. 2 Chronicles 35:18
66. 2 Chronicles 34:6, 9
67. 2 Chronicles 30:6, 9-11, 18
68. 2 Kings 24:14-15
69. Jeremiah 37:10
70. 2 Kings 25:13
71. Jeremiah 40:4
72. Jeremiah 43:5-6
73. Jeremiah 43:5-6
74. Amos 9:8-9
75. 1 Nephi 22:4; 2 Nephi 10:22
76. Jeremiah 16:16
77. Deuteronomy 33:17
78. Joseph Smith, *History of the Church of Jesus Christ of Latter-day Saints* (Salt Lake City: Deseret Book Company), Vol. 1, pp. 11-12.
79. *Ibid.*, pp. 15-16.
80. *Ibid.*, pp 39-40.
81. *Ibid.*, Vol. 4, p. 541.
82. 1 Corinthians 15:39-42
83. Doctrine and Covenants 76:62-68, 70
84. Doctrine and Covenants 88:22
85. 2 Corinthians 12:2
86. John 3:5
87. Brigham Young, *Journal of Discourses* (London: Latter-day Saints Book Depot, 1855), Vol. 2, p 31
88. Joseph Fielding Smith (comp.), *Teachings of the Prophet Joseph Smith* (Salt Lake City: Deseret Book Company, 1976),   p. 345
89. Abraham 3:2-4
90. Joseph Smith, *History of the Church of Jesus Christ of Latter-day Saints* (Salt Lake City: Deseret Book Company),   Vol. 1, pp 3-5
91. 1 John 10:16
92. 3 Nephi 15:21; 16:1-3; 17:4
93. Doctrine and Covenants 133:26-27
94. Doctrine and Covenants 133:30-34
95. Jeremiah 7:15
96. Doctrine and Covenants 133:20-25
97. Isaiah 29:14; Ezekiel 33:33.
98. Romans 9:6.

About the Author

Clay McConkie is a native of Utah. He is a teacher by occupation, having taught in the Salt Lake City Schools for thirty years. He received a B.A. from Brigham Young University and an M.S. and Ph. D. from the University of Utah. He and his wife reside in Provo, Utah, and they are the parents of four children.

He is also the author of *The Ten Lost Tribes, One Flesh,* and *The Gathering of the Waters.*